THE ILLUSTRATED HISTORY

GINETTA

THE ILLUSTRATED HISTORY

John Rose

Foulis

Haynes

To my late parents

ISBN 0 85429 384 1

First published 1983
A FOULIS Motoring Book
Copyright John Rose 1983

Published by:
Haynes Publishing Group
Sparkford, Yeovil, Somerset BA22 7JJ *England*

Distributed in North America by:
Haynes Publications inc.
861 Lawrence Drive, Newbury Park,
California 91320 USA

Printed in England by: J. H. Haynes & Co. Ltd.

Frontispiece: The four Walklett brothers pose cheerfully
with a single-seater Ginetta G17
Left to right: Douglas, Ivor, Bob, and Trevers

Although Trevers' name appears throughout this book as 'Trevor', and he is known as 'Trevor',
the above is, in fact, the correct spelling of his name.

CONTENTS

Bob Walklett introduces Lord Snowdon to the convertible Ginetta G10 at the 1965 Racing Car Show

FOREWORD

by Bob Walklett

WHEN John Rose asked me if I would like to write the Foreword to his book, he explained that it would be a fully illustrated record of the many racing and sports cars Ginetta have produced over the past twenty-five years. Naturally, his opinions and conclusions are his own, but John has fully achieved what he set out to do.

I think Ivor is currently the best UK sports car designer around, and I have yet to hear of anyone who can match Trevers' flair for translating a design into a reasonable-looking prototype in such a short time. Douglas, perhaps, has performed the hardest task, through being responsible for the 'in-between' work which, of course, makes the whole thing possible.

Readers of this book will not need reminding of the high casualty rate amongst the specialist car manufacturers. We have shared the same minefield and survived.

What of the future? Well, I think our experience and expertise, gained over the past twenty-five years, will ensure that there are more Ginetta models in the years to come. I hope you enjoy this book.

Bob Walklett
Managing Director, Ginetta Cars Ltd

ACKNOWLEDGEMENTS

The author is indebted to the following people whose help and assistance made this book possible.

Bob Walklett, managing director of Ginetta Cars Ltd; Steve Greensword, secretary of the Ginetta Owners' Club; Trevor Pyman, registrar of the Ginetta Owners' Club; Peter Dixon, registrar of the Historic and Sports Car Club; David Polglaze, competition secretary of the Historic and Sports Car Club; Peter 'Leigh' Davis, Steve Newport, Richard A Petit, David Beams, Ian Higgins, Tony Clinkard, John Morris, Derek Buckett, Roger Davis, Dick Ellingham, Peter Voigt, Alan Hailey, Brian Moody, Gerry Tyack, Richard Homer, Peter Cook, Ian Bax, Keith Jones, Rod Leach, Donald Grant, Malcolm Elston, Neil Emery, Andy Woolley, David Atkins, Katsuji Yoshida, Bruno Meir, Marcel Spiess, Hans Braun, Russell Madden, and the many members of the Ginetta Owners' Club who have encouraged me throughout the duration of this venture.

I would also like to thank *Classic & Sportscar*, *Autosport*, *Motoring News*, *Road & Track* USA, *Cars and Car Conversions*, *Alternative Cars Ltd*, *Motor Sport*, and *Thoroughbred and Classic Car* for their very helpful co-operation.

Last, but not least, to my very good friend and colleague, Tom Colverson — retired publishing lecturer of some repute — whose help and expertise was invaluable.

	Colour plates	Photographer					
1	G4, Peter Dixon	*Hugo Dixon*	4	G12, Richard A Petit	*Richard A Petit*	7	G22, Works car	*Steve Greensword*
2	G4, Tony Clinkard	*Fred Scatley*	5	G16, Peter Cook	*Derek Hibbert*	8	G23, Steve Newport	*Steve Newport*
3	G11, John Rose	*John Rose*	6	G17, Richard Homer	*Derek Hibbert*			

Tony Clinkard, an active Ginetta G4 competitor, seen here leading a Lotus Europa, MG Midget, and a G15, during a race at Snetterton in May 1982

Peter Dixon — Registrar of the Historic and Sports Car Club, and an avid Ginetta enthusiast — competing in his Ginetta G4

Rear view of the author's MGB-engined Ginetta G11 coupé. Thought to be the only remaining coupé in the UK — in virtually its original condition

Ultra-smooth, Ferrari-like lines, dominate designer Richard Petit's beautiful, one-off, Ginetta G12.

Peter Cook in his totally immaculate, record-breaking, Ginetta G16.

Superbly prepared and immaculate, the much modified, ex-Peter Voigt, Imp-powered Ginetta G17 of Richard Homer

The attractive Ginetta G22 Sports 2000 racer in the Witham showroom. Sadly, it was abandoned and consequently never appeared on the circuits in a race.

The extremely fast, Ford 2.8-litre V6, convertible G23, with its somewhat unusual, but very distinctive, hardtop in position.

INTRODUCTION

Ginetta Cars Ltd, of Witham in Essex, must surely rate as the most remarkable of the specialist car manufacturers. Against all the odds this small company has managed to stay in business for the past twenty-five years, building their attractive road and racing cars. In fact, Ginetta are not only remarkable but possibly unique. Of all the small specialist car manufacturers, they were probably the only firm not to have gone through what was an almost compulsory bankruptcy phase during the economic crisis of the early 1970s. And after all these years, the four brothers who formed the company are still at the helm today, firmly established in the quiet country town of Witham.

An important contributory factor to their survival is, perhaps, that the business is well and truly a 'family affair'. The brothers consist of Bob, as managing director; Ivor, on design; Trevor, on chassis; and Douglas, as works manager.

The brothers' philosophy is, and always has been, to use the simple, straightforward approach, and to do things *their* way.

During these many years the Walkletts have never sought the limelight, and have generally kept a low profile. It has never been their style to splash out with masses of advertising, but meanwhile they have built up a devoted following of enthusiasts, worldwide, with their excellent marque. As for the origin of the name 'Ginetta': to this day that has been the brothers' best-kept secret; it remains a mystery.

1

Ginetta at the 1966
Racing Car Show
l-r, G11, G4, G12

Chapter One

ENTHUSIASTIC BEGINNINGS

Ginetta G1 (1957)

IT was in the early 1950s, before the formation of Ginetta Cars, that the Walklett brothers were running an agricultural and constructional engineering business at Campsea Ashe, a few miles from Woodbridge in Suffolk. Throughout this period they could frequently be found at Snetterton, their local motor racing circuit, all four brothers being avid motor racing enthusiasts.

This shared enthusiasm for racing cars gave Ivor Walklett the impetus to experiment with some chassis designs he had drawn up. The brothers' business meant that all necessary raw materials were readily to hand, so Ivor set about putting his theories into practice. With assistance from his brothers, Ivor decided that the basis for his project would be an old pre-war Wolseley Hornet that happened to be in the brothers' possession at that time, the mid-fifties.

The Wolseley Hornet was dismantled, the chassis meticulously restored and various improvements were made at the same time. Ivor then returned to his drawing board and designed a new body for the chassis. From his designs he made and put together an all-aluminium body which, when fitted, resulted in a car somewhat resembling a 4CLT Maserati. This car was entered and driven in several motor club events. Its life was not long, however, as the car, later to be known as the Ginetta G1, sadly came to a sticky end. Apparently, the Walkletts had this very long driveway to their house — it had a couple of bends and a hairpin! Ivor came home one day in the car, his thoughts obviously elsewhere, careered straight through some bushes and was halted by an uncompromising tree stump! Consequently 'G1' was a total write-off and the remains that could be salvaged were sold.

It was this spare-time enterprise and enthusiasm that was to see the making of a budding designer and sports/racing car manufacturer.

Do-it-yourself sports car, the first production Ginetta — the G2

Chapter Two

INTO PRODUCTION

Ginetta G2 (1958–1960)

IVOR'S modified Wolseley Hornet, later known as the Ginetta G1, had certainly kindled the brothers' enthusiasm: so much so that it was decided that they would build a car for sale to the motoring enthusiast. Basically, the aim was to provide for the enthusiast with limited means a fast, economical and practical 2-seater sports car at low cost. To achieve this goal the car had to be designed primarily for the home constructor who possessed no equipment other than the usual handful of tools.

Ivor Walklett carried out the initial work and designed a simple multi-tubular space-frame chassis comprising 1-inch O.D. 16 and 18 SWG steel tubing. A 20 gauge aluminium body was then made to clothe the chassis. The bulkhead, floor, body panels and propshaft tunnel were all fixed permanently to the chassis frame, making for an extremely rigid unit. Cycle-type wings shielded all four wheels and the finished car was called the Ginetta G2.

The G2 would accept either the Ford 8 h.p or 10 h.p. vehicle components (1938–1953) and the recently introduced Ford Popular E93A engine and running gear. Four modifications were deemed necessary, these being the lengthening of the steering column, the shortening of the propshaft and the alteration of the radius arms, and the gear lever. Ginetta themselves would undertake to do these modifications at a small extra charge if required, although suggesting at the same time that it would be preferable to use a new steering column and box, already lengthened, which they could supply at a cost of £9 10s. The factory also offered other modifications such as IFS on swing-axle principle. The approximate weight of the body-frame was 150lb. This included adjustable clutch and brake pedals with linkage, accelerator pedal, mounting brackets for the engine, steering, radiator, petrol tank, axles and so on — all of which were built in.

A completed G2 had a wheelbase of 7 feet 6 inches and an equal front and rear track of 3 feet 9 inches. Excluding the spare wheel, its overall dimensions were: length, 10 feet 6 inches; height to scuttle, 2 feet 5 inches; height to top of hood, 3 feet 8 inches. The weight was just over 8 cwt.

At the beginning of 1958, in conjunction with their agricultural engineering business, Ginetta Cars was formed. The Ginetta G2 was put into limited production at a cost of £156 ex works. This price was for the basic body/chassis frame and included four wings, the nose cowl and bonnet cover. The final cost of putting the car on the road depended entirely on whether the enthusiast used new or secondhand components. The use of new parts alone would have resulted in a total price of not less than £486. However, by using mainly secondhand components it was possible to complete a G2 for less than £250. Several motoring magazines featured the

just introduced their new 997cc OHV 105E power unit.

Taking into consideration these advances, the Walkletts decided that they would take advantage of this material and go ahead and build a glassfibre car which could utilise the new 105E engine.

Around 100 examples of the G2 model were produced between 1958 and its demise in 1960. Very few still survive today.

The partly restored G2 of 'Leigh' Davis won 1st prize in the 'specials' class at Southern Sidevalve day held at the Cotswold Wildlife Park 1981

Rear view of a G2

new car and with some combined advertisement coverage the brothers suddenly found themselves in real business: so much so, in fact, that by the middle of the year the Walkletts had plumped to put half their concern into building cars on a full-time basis.

For eighteen months the G2 had sold steadily, but it was beginning to be hampered by its appearance. The age of the Ford Special was now in full swing, with many enthusiasts fitting attractive-looking, but frail, glassfibre bodies to their Ford Popular chassis. Moreover, Ford, whose engines were extremely popular with the 'special' and racing fraternity, had

The first glassfibre bodied Ginetta — the G3, with its hardtop in position

8

Chapter Three

FOLLOWING THE TREND

Ginetta G3 (1960–1962)

NOW was the era of the kit car, with more and more enthusiasts resolving to build their own cars. Glassfibre was beginning to be widely used for specialist car bodies and this led the Walklett brothers to design their first car for sale with a body made of this material.

This car, which would be called the Ginetta G3, had its chassis constructed along similar lines to that of its predecessor, the G2. Once again the idea was to allow the enthusiast to strip certain components from his old car and bolt them to the new chassis. With the G3 this was made a straightforward procedure by providing all attachment points and pre-drilling all holes. The multi-tubular structure of the chassis once again made this an extremely rigid and strong unit.

As with the G2, this car was also built to accept Ford 8 hp and 10 hp components (1938–1953) or, if required, Ford Popular components (1953 on-wards) including the newly introduced Ford 997 105E unit. The chassis included retention of the rear radius arms and was fitted with an independent front suspension conversion, comprising coil springs and telescopic dampers. Also fitted were rear telescopic dampers, floor and propshaft tunnel.

The moulded glassfibre body had an exceptionally smooth surface, free of the ripples commonly found at the time in glassfibre bodies. A very comprehensive list of items was included: all locks, hinges and handles were ready fitted. All wing-edges were rebated or turned-in (a refinement that some specialists tended to ignore) and the wheel arches were bonded in. Flat surfaces were provided to allow the fitment of rear lights, indicators and registration plates. A boot was built in, as were the front and rear bulkheads, with reinforced scuttle at the sides and also a built-in tube was supplied to facilitate location of the steering column. Bumpers

Doug Lowry racing his modified G3 at Mosport, Ontario, Canada in 1982

The neatly modified G3 of brothers John and Keith Morris, who competed the car in hillclimbs during the 1970s

Engine access!

also were built in, as was the fascia panel, an occasional rear seat (incidentally this could be used by children) and much more, making it a very comprehensive package indeed.

A hardtop was included to allow a choice of fixed or open motoring. Access for occupants was made easy by large, fully opening doors which were complete with interior trim panels. Engine access was made ridiculously easy by hingeing the complete front end. This, however, looked somewhat precarious as the whole bonnet section hinged and opened rearwards (similar to the 'Frogeye' Sprite), giving one visions of any mechanic working on the engine suddenly being gobbled up if he accidentally displaced the long bonnet stay.

The Ginetta G3 had an all-enveloping body and

this looked very sleek, showing some resemblance to an early AC Ace or Cobra.

The G3 sold well in component form for some two years.

Chapter Four

A RACING CERTAINTY

Ginetta G4 (1961–1969) incorporating G5/G6/G7

WHILST the company had been building and selling the G3, Ivor Walklett, who once again had carried out most of the design and development work, had been quietly busy, engaged on the next project. This time he had designed a really remarkable Ginetta, destined to become one the most famous of the marque. The successor was the Ginetta G4: a dual-purpose sports car, suitable for everyday use but also able to give the owner the opportunity to partake in club racing.

Although this was originally planned to accept a production version of the Climax 750cc power unit, lack of orders for the engine from other specialists meant that Ginetta had to look elsewhere for a power unit. Eventually they decided to play safe and stick to the Ford 997cc unit.

Finishing touches were put to the new car and the Ginetta G4 (Series I) was unveiled to the public at the 1961 Racing Car Show, held at the Horticultural Halls, Westminster, London. The Walklett brothers must have been delighted as the car aroused immense interest and actually received the accolade of 'best looking car of the show'.

The basis of the G4 was a multi-tubular space-frame chassis of triangulated construction using 1-inch x 18 gauge round steel tube, with square steel tubing used at the suspension mounting points. The frame itself was cut down at the sides of the cockpit, forming a high sill to allow the doors to be fitted. Eccentric double wishbone and coil-spring/damper units of Ginetta design were employed for the front suspension; at the rear a Ford Anglia live axle was located by trailing arms and an 'A' bracket, also with coil-spring/damper units.

The glassfibre body was flattering with low frontal area and Lotus Eleven-like tail fins at the rear, giving an appearance which proved to be very popular. The body was made up with the scuttle section

The first Ginetta G4 Series 1, unveiled in 1961

leaving space for little more than a medium-sized holdall.

The G4 was made available in partly assembled form at an initial cost of £697 and although the car's interior trim was somewhat sparse the price did include all the parts necessary to complete a car. The attractive glassfibre body was supplied with the centre section bonded to the chassis frame, the forward-hinging bonnet and detachable tail section, floor, bulkheads, wheel arches and doors all fitted before leaving the works. The lockable boot did not have its floor fitted as standard, however, thus enabling the competition-minded owner to gain easy access to the rear axle and battery.

The kit came complete with all suspension parts ready assembled. A set of instruments was included, comprising speedometer, fuel and water temperature gauges, and all necessary switches, plus all other components including seats, windscreen (from a Mark I Sprite), five wheels and tyres — and, of course, a hood. This had to be erected on an ingenious arrangement of hoodsticks but proved fully weatherproof when fitted.

The statistics of the Series I G4 were: overall length, 11 feet; scuttle height, 2 feet 3 inches; height to top of screen, 3 feet 1 inch; width, 4 feet 8 inches; wheelbase, 6 feet 8 inches; and a front and rear track of 3 feet 10 inches. 13-inch pressed steel wheels were used. The car weighed around 8¾ cwt.

It was not long before the Walkletts reduced the

bonded to the chassis tubes. The complete bonnet section, held by two spring clips, hinged forward in Triumph Herald style and both bonnet and boot were quickly detachable after releasing six bolts, four at the rear and two at the front. This easy removal provided for superb accessibility and, of course, much simplified panel replacement in the event of any damage received in an accident. The double-skinned doors were troublesome to open as, like the original MG 'A' and Sprite, they did not possess any external handles. Because the G4 was designed with performance uppermost, this left little room to spare, making it strictly a two-seater sports car. The boot, which already held the 5-gallon glassfibre fuel tank (it was necessary to unlock the boot to replenish as there was no external filler cap), also held the spare wheel and weather-equipment, price of a complete kit to a moderate £499. The hood and sidescreens were now extra, however, as was painting the body. For only an extra £16 the customer could specify the Ford Classic 1340cc engine or even higher states of tune. It was not a surprise that the G4 began to sell extremely well at this modest price.

To continue their development programme the Walkletts decided that they needed larger premises. So just one year after the launch of the Ginetta G4, Ginetta Cars Limited moved from their premises in Suffolk to take over a moderately-sized garage and works at one end of the small but pleasant Essex town of Witham, near Chelmsford. Simultaneously, the four brothers had decided to put all their efforts into building cars on a full-time basis.

The G4 came in for its first updating in early 1963. The Series II G4 dispensed with the Lotus Eleven-like tail and was replaced by a vastly improved tail section looking even sleeker. At the same time this enabled the boot to be given more capacity. Annoyingly, the boot still had to be opened to permit access to the fuel filler, although this was later changed and situated on the outside of the body.

One of the very few remaining early tail Series 1 G4s. This pristine example, owned by Ray Dibben, won the award of 'best-preserved GT' at the 1982 Hindhead kit-car rally

The new tail was also given a more modern slab rear end and the car's overall length had thereby increased by some 8 inches. Various other changes were made to improve the car. The Ford Anglia rear axle had been found to be somewhat limited with its small number of ratios available; and to remedy this situation a BMC unit was installed which not only had a far wider range of final drive ratios, but was also some 40lb lighter in weight. This had the added advantage of enabling different coil-spring rates to be used, resulting in much improved ride characteristics.

Chris Meek was the works driver, and was immensely successful in his G4, with records galore

The front suspension was also modified at the same time. The bottoms of the spring/damper units were moved outwards towards the apex of the bottom wishbone above the trunnion pivot, thus im-

G4s in various stages of assembly in the Ginetta workshops

Cockpit of the G4 — note chassis rails along bottom of door opening

proving the effectiveness of the damper and at the same time increasing the spring-to-suspension travel ratio. The car also had the option of a hardtop with a built-in curved laminated windscreen and perspex rear and side screens.

Although 8-inch drum brakes had been used and found to be perfectly adequate, front wheel disc brakes were made available as an option at very little extra cost. This was much appreciated by the competition-minded customer, for whom also a lightweight car was to be produced using a thin laminated bodyshell. The saving in weight did not, however, justify the extra trouble incurred, so this venture was not continued.

17

Neatly installed, and very accessible engine bay

For those who wanted their engines in a higher state of tune, Ginetta would modify the 997cc engine at reasonable cost, but always recommended those looking for ultimate power output to go to one of the leading tuning firms.

The sales of the G4 increased. On 5th September 1963, the 997cc G4 was homologated for International Racing, the company having produced the one hundred identically-engined cars necessary to comply with regulations. Now the club racing fraternity were beginning to show more interest. The G4 offered good potential and also some refinement which the Lotus Seven did not have.

The potential of the G4 on the circuit was soon realised when a number of G4 drivers actually

The 'G5', or rather a G4 fitted with a Cortina 1498cc engine, with its Series 2 bodywork and optional hardtop

18

began winning races. And none more so than one Nick Grace from London who was trouncing the opposition in his 997cc-engined G4, notching up win after win. One particular race at Goodwood not only saw him win but saw him also take the lap record at 1 minute 38 seconds (88.16 mph) with virtually no opposition.

Another racing driver who became attracted to the G4 was Chris Meek. He personally thought that the car could take a lot more power. Not wasting any time he had a G4 built to racing specifications whilst he himself was building his own 1650cc pushrod Ford engine with Cosworth camshaft. The engine was subsequently installed in the Ginetta when it arrived. Meek asked Bob Walklett for support from the factory and after some very impressive drives in his G4, Chris Meek eventually became the works driver, an arrangement that was to last for many years.

1964 saw Meek have an outstanding season of racing in his G4, gaining no fewer than eight wins and six second placings. In August of the same year he broke the lap record at Snetterton for GT cars up to 2,500cc. This record had previously been held by the powerful Porsche 904 of Dickee Stoop. Meek had lapped at 1 minute 46.2 seconds (91.86 mph). This success saw the G4R (Racing) evolve, an all-round disc-braked version using independent rear suspension — an option, incidentally, for road-going G4s as well.

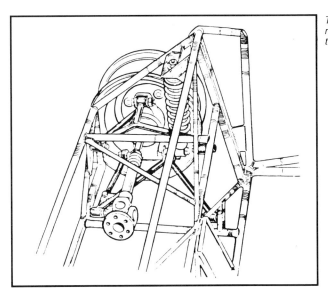

The independent rear suspension of the G4 'R'

Chris Meek in the works G4 at Mallory Park

Its success in racing also contributed to increased sales of road-going G4s including a new, more powerfully engined, version. The Walkletts had taken advantage of the introduction of the new Ford 1498cc OHV Cortina power unit. With this engine installed in the G4 the car was announced as the new 'G5'. However, the designation G5 led to all sorts of problems as everyone, including the Walkletts, kept referring to it as the G4. Finally, it all got so confusing that the designation was dropped altogether and was referred to from then on as the G4 '1500'.

The G4 continued to be a sensation in motor racing, especially in the hands of Chris Meek in the works car. One race that comes immediately to

This shot shows the much sleeker tail of the Series 2 G4

mind was at Snetterton in May, 1966. Meek drove a phenomenal practice session, coming in six seconds faster than Gerry Marshall in a TVR Griffith. Amazingly, his time was also faster than any of the Formula Three cars had been able to put in during the day. The actual race itself turned out to be even more exciting, with Meek eventually taking the chequered flag and seemingly every spectator on his feet roaring approval. By coincidence that day also saw another G4, this time in the hands of one John Burton, set fastest time of the day at Loton Park hillclimb. Another driver who was breaking the lap records on the circuits was Johnny Blades, a Whitley Bay shopkeeper. Between 1965 and 1968 his 1650cc G4 held the lap record, for GT cars up to 2,500cc, at Croft Autodrome.

The Walkletts, meanwhile, had continued with further development on the G4. Stronger Mark II Triumph front uprights and stub axles had superseded the earlier set-up and the brake callipers were moved to the rear of the discs. The original Ginetta made eccentric top and bottom front wishbones were replaced by the standard Triumph concentric pressed steel wishbones and the BMC Mini steering rack that had been utilised, was changed for a left-hand-drive unit, mounted upside down and positioned to the front of the wheels (instead of to the rear). The optional hardtop was altered to accommodate a more intensely raked windscreen (the same screen as fitted to the G12). This enhanced the aerodynamic curves of the G4 even more and later the hardtop was in fact incorporated into the body-work, turning the car into a coupé.

Other detail changes pensued including a new cockpit fascia, the centre console was lowered to meet the gearbox tunnel and padded bucket seats replaced the foam cushions and one-piece back-rests.

However, by far the most significant alteration was to the chassis itself. The new chassis was of

Gerry Hunt, Far East GT champion, poses with his very successful G4 and some of his trophies

Peter 'Leigh' Davis in his first-ever race at Silverstone 1967

Albrecht Mantzel, wizard German engineer, with one of the specially adapted DKW-engined G6s, at the start of the 1963 1000 Kilometres race at Nurburgring

21

similar design in so far as it was also a multi-tubular spaceframe with the glassfibre body resin-bonded to it, but this time far less tubing was used and square steel tube of 1-inch and 1½-inch x 18 gauge was used as opposed to the earlier round steel tube of 1-inch x 18 gauge.

The final changes to the G4 came in 1966 and was marketed as the Series III G4. For compliance with the new headlamp height regulations a new bonnet section was made and fitted with flip-up type units. The car was made to look even more refined by the addition of a front bumper, external handles

Ready for the off, in the 1000 Kilometres race at Nurburgring. The G6 was driven by Albrecht's son, Dieter Mantzel, and also Peter Ruby — both DKW works drivers

22

on the doors for the first time and reshaped, braced side-windows, and the cockpit was fully carpeted. As can be seen in the photograph of the car at the 1966 Racing Car Show, the G4 Series III was really sleek looking.

Variations on the G4 had extended to the G6 and G7. In fact the G6 was simply a G4 modified to take a three-cylinder, 850cc two-stroke DKW engine. All that had been required was a change of engine mountings and springs. Only three examples of this designation were built and these were made specifically for a German engineer by the name of Albrecht Mantzel, who had ordered the cars after meeting the Walkletts at the 1961 Racing Car Show. One G6 was in fact entered in the 1963 1000 Kilometre race at the Nurburgring and driven by Albrecht's son, Dieter Mantzel, and also Peter Ruby — both were works drivers for DKW. The car performed extremely well but unfortunately failed to complete the race. The G7 was a prototype which was again a variation on the standard G4. However, this derivative utilised a transaxle at the rear instead of the conventional forward-mounted gearbox and separate axle at the rear. This was done mainly as a bit of pioneering and experimentation in the interest of weight distribution. Rear-engined cars had been virtually unheard of at the time. The car could have been well suited for events such as hillclimbs but the plan was shelved when only the prototype had been built.

Ginetta's US importer raced his own G4 in the States. Here he lines up next to a Ferrari on the front row of the grid

'Leigh' again, this time at Barcelona in 1971

23

24

Production of the G4 continued up until 1969 and although other models of the marque were being built and sold during this period it was the G4 that had been the mainstay of the company and its road to success — well over 500 cars having been built at its demise.

The finalising of production, however, did not see the end of the success of the G4. During the early 1970s John Absalom from Northumberland raced

Porsche Speedster, driven by world champion rally driver Walter Rohrl, closely followed by Hans Braun in his Ginetta G4. Hans, in fact, went on to beat Rohrl in this particular race.

'Leigh' Davis lapping a Lotus 23B on GP circuit at Silverstone, 1967

Hans Braun, a G4 enthusiast, who competes regularly in Germany

his modified G4 in the newly formed Modsports series and at one time held virtually every northern lap record. No less than a dozen wins were credited to John during the season of 1971. The list of successes was to continue. And the success was not confined to this country alone. The diminutive G4 has graced racetracks across the globe: Nurburgring, Sebring, Spa, Singapore, Trinidad — to name but a few. Ginetta's US importer raced his own G4 in the States. Gerry Hunt became Far East GT Champion

Tony Clinkard in competitive spirit, minus the front end of his G4, during a 750 MC 6-hour relay race

Bill Higgins in his G4 at Croft in 1978 pictured after an off and just re-passing the Lotus Elan of Peter Lee

27

Ian Higgins' G4 at Donington 1978, side by side with an Elan. Ian finished 2nd overall and set the fastest lap

Ian at Snetterton 1981, 2nd overall and fastest lap again. Ian finished 2nd overall in Garelli sports cars championship and 1st overall in Garelli modified sports cars

with his G4. Even the Irish GT Championship was won twice by Norman Moffett in his G4.

Over the years many others have campaigned the G4, including John and George Gould, Peter 'Leigh' Davis, John Burton, David Cameron, David Atkins, Peter Bryan, Roy Stanley, Eric Walker, Ian Bax, Eddie Falkous, David Mercer, Tony Herbert, Tony Clinkard, Bob Cook, Mike Chittenden and his partner Fred Taylor, Peter Dixon, John Digby, Ian and Bill Higgins, Arthur Kellitt, Hans Braun, Magnus Neergard, Dick Ellingham, John Wilmshurst, John H. Haynes, Jeremy Rossiter, Edward Wong, Alan

The modified G4 of Ian Bax and John Wilmshurst. Between them, they gained many wins during 1977. More recently, this same car has been raced by John Digby— with considerable success.

The above car again, but now much modified

29

The Alan Milchard entered G4, driven by David Atkins, in an STP modsports round at Mallory Park during 1972

Minshaw, and the Douglas brothers. And so one could go on: the list is almost endless. The Walkletts' little wonder continues to thrill on the racetracks even today. Many G4s fitted with Ford 1600cc twin-cam engines, made eligible in 1974, were and still are successful in Modsports races and one can still see road-going G4s entered in their respective classes.

Of all the G4 driver/enthusiasts, Peter 'Leigh' Davis of Evesham, Worcs, perhaps deserves a special mention. He owns not one, but two G4s, and is presently in the midst of restoring an ancient G2. One of the G4s, LAC 64E, had become synonymous

with Peter, who has owned the car since he purchased it new in 1966. Peter is deeply involved in his motor sport and has raced both his G4s at many, many circuits, home and abroad — among those he has competed in include the 1972 Targa Florio, and the Barcelona 1000 Kilometres. Unfortunately, he and his co-driver, Roger Andreason, had to retire from the latter race, held in October 1971, after going extremely well for five hours when they were lying in twelfth position, because of two broken exhaust valves.

But it was only recently that Peter and LAC 64E really hit the headlines, when he became the first known person to enter a G4 in a major rally — and the Himalayan Rally at that! Although he and his co-driver, Roger Mugeridge, failed to complete the gruelling rally, the G4 attracted more attention than any other car in the rally, and it was widely exposed in the motoring media that covered the event. Indians, in their hordes, would constantly surround the little G4, which they apparently nick-named 'the bathtub', prodding the glassfibre body and whispering 'plastic, plastic' among themselves.

Not content with previous achievements, Peter is now ambitious to compete his G4 in the marathon Peking to Paris Motoring Challenge.

And so to conclude, the Ginetta G4 has become a legend in itself and without question this very fine dual-purpose sports car has proved to be one of the most successful since the mid-forties.

31

Manufacturing difficulties put paid to the attractive G8 single-seater Formula 3 car

32

Chapter Five

SINGLE-SEATER RACER

Ginetta G8 (1964) incorporating G9

IT was during 1964, whilst production of the G4 continued, that Ivor and Trevor Walklett, who between them were now responsible for the design and chassis work, came up with the Ginetta G8. This was a rather unusual, if not quite unique, glassfibre monocoque single-seater Formula Three racing car.

The uppermost priority was to produce a totally rigid chassis. It soon became apparent, however, that the process involved in putting together the Ginetta G8 entailed incredible precision. Two glassfibre shells were bonded together over a perimeter steel tube chassis, thus producing an immensely strong monocoque. But the delicate operation required at least six workers to locate the two shells together by hand. Even the tiniest error at this critical bonding stage rendered the unit unusable as it was impossible to apply any rectification beyond this point.

Nevertheless, three Ginetta G8s were completed

and Chris Meek, the works driver, drove one to a creditable fourth place on the car's first outing in a race at Snetterton, but the venture was shelved because of the aforementioned manufacturing difficulties.

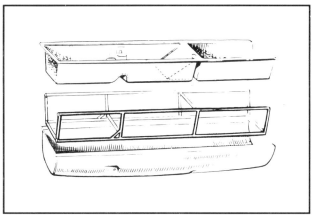

Two glassfibre shells were bonded together over a steel chassis

A similar venture to build a Formula Two racing car which had been in the pipeline was also halted at the same time. This would, in fact, have been designated the G9, but the company wanted to turn its attention back to GT cars. And this is what the brothers did.

Chapter Six

POTENTIAL MONEY-SPINNERS

Ginetta G10 and G11 (1965–1966)

THE four brothers resolved to stay in the area which they considered to be their special territory, that of making GT cars. Ivor was given the initial design task and from the drawing board on this occasion he came up with a real cracker of a car — the Ginetta G10!

This appeared initially as an extremely powerful 2-seater road-going car, powered by an almighty American Ford 4.7-litre V8 engine, its primary objectives being the American market and competition for the AC Cobra.

Evolving round a semi-spaceframe chassis, with the glassfibre body bonded to it, the Ginetta G10 was very much larger than previous Ginetta models. Utilising a Ford 4-speed and reverse gearbox, with synchromesh on all forward gears, it had all-round independent suspension comprising coil springs and telescopic dampers, with disc-brakes on all four wheels. The front discs were 11½-inch diameter,

mounted outboard, while those at the rear were 10½-inch, mounted inboard, alongside a Salisbury limited-slip differential (as used on Jaguars). Dual-brake master cylinders were employed to ensure that there was always some means of slowing the brute — which had a reputed 271 bhp, giving a top speed in the region of 150 mph. The G10 was an extremely strong car, but at the same time was reasonably light in weight.

The Ginetta G10 was made public at the 1965 Racing Car Show held in London at Olympia. Its appearance had admirers remarking that it resembled a 'big MGB'. Comments along these lines were readily understandable, especially when one realised that it used steel doors which were, in fact, complete original MGB items, as were the windscreen and the hood on the convertible example exhibited. A fixed-head coupé was introduced soon afterwards which employed specially made front

The works G10 convertible on its debut in the hands of Chris Meek

and rear laminated screens, thus making this version look much less like an MGB.

By all accounts the G10 was probably ahead of its time and, fully built, it had a price tag of £2,729. Its interior was fairly refined for the period with well-shaped, adjustable and reclining bucket seats, smart wood-rimmed steering wheel, full carpeting and trim and, of course, wind-up windows. An array of gauges and switches gave the necessary information and took care of things like lights, washers, wipers, fan and so on. In front of the Ginetta badge on the boss of the steering wheel was a rev-counter, and a speedometer which read up to 220 mph! This could have been considered a status symbol in itself!

Later that year the convertible G10 was tried in competition when it was entered in a sports car race at Brands Hatch. Chris Meek was once again given the opportunity to drive a Ginetta on its competition debut. Spectators at the race were left gasping as the big Ginetta simply powered home to a convincing win against opposition that included E-type Jaguars — and this was with a basically undeveloped car!

The Walkletts did enjoy initial orders from the United States which were to form the first small batch of a much larger requirement for the American importer. The G10 was intended for use in American GT races, but when it was learned that the SCCA (Sports Car Club of America) had included the G10 in with sports racing cars, such as McLaren's and Lola's, because the G10 had not been homologated, and not in GT racing, the Walklett brothers received cancellations from the American importer, as the car would not have been competitive against such opposition. So production of a car that could have been a real success was halted after only six cars had been completed. Four of these were fastback hardtops and two were convertibles.

The demise of the G10 had many enthusiasts asking Bob Walklett why the car couldn't be kept going for the home market alone, perhaps by utilising a smaller power unit? The brothers reviewed the situation and, taking into account the large number of enquiries they were receiving, concluded that it would be a sound idea, and that as parts were already being supplied by BMC it would seem sensible to fit the engine, gearbox and live axle from the MGB itself.

Work commenced and the Ginetta G11 was born. Bodily it looked exactly like the G10, but without the power bulge in the bonnet, and it was

The classic, very powerful, and attractive Ginetta G10 coupé

Rod Leach described his G10 as the fastest accelerating road car he has ever driven—including 7-litre Cobras!

Rod's G10 ahead of a Cobra!

4727cc Ford V8—430 bhp—in the G10 owned by Rod Leach, after a multi-thousand £ restoration

Smart and purposeful interior

launched at the 1966 Racing Car Show. Once again, as with the G10, it was to be made available as a fixed-head or in a convertible guise. The public's reaction was splendid, making the G11 a very popular specialist sports car. It is understood that the G11 had probably the most demand of any car ever built by Ginetta.

The glassfibre body was bonded to the chassis exactly as was that of the G10. The same MGB steel doors were again used, a somewhat unusual feature of an otherwise all-glassfibre body. The front suspension was independent, comprising transverse wishbones, coil springs and telescopic dampers and an anti-roll bar of Ginetta design. Steering was rack and pinion, contrived from the Austin Mini. At the rear the live axle was located by an 'A' bracket and radius arms, with coil springs and telescopic dam-

Russell Madden's G11 with an MGB hardtop and some added glamour!

*G11 convertible
body/chassis*

pers, and for braking the G11 had 9½-inch discs fitted at the front, whilst 10-inch diameter MGB drums coped with the rear. Sixty-spoke wire wheels (4½-inch x 14-inch), fitted with Dunlop R35 Roadspeed nylon tyres, were used to give the coupé a more classic look.

Interior trim of the fixed-head coupé was somewhat special, with reclining two-tone Restall seats with tilt-forward mechanisms. The convertible used bucket seats, although both versions were fully car-

*Immaculate G11
convertible*

Alternative Cars Ltd

40

peted and had a comprehensive range of instruments fitted. Luggage space on the platform behind the seats, although deep, was limited by the rake of the rear screen and also by its being of the same height as the top of the propshaft tunnel. Nevertheless, a reasonable amount of luggage could be carried. The very deep boot was dominated by the 10-gallon fuel tank and spare wheel, but still had enough room for those essential items.

Although the closed version of the G11 had

The author's G11 coupé, thought to be the only one remaining in the UK in almost original condition

(in the background is the author's G15)

mouldings to which rear quarter-bumpers were fixed, the convertible had none. Some G10 coupés had quarter-bumpers all round. Both versions used curved perspex covers over the headlights.

Using the 4-cylinder 1798cc OHV MGB engine and gearbox, the G11 had a top speed of 110 mph and a reputed 95 bhp. Its cruising speed was 88 mph and it could return an average of 28 mpg. Fuel replenishment was made simple by an outwardly mounted, quick-release, flip-up filler-cap.

At this point, perhaps it is fair to say that another reason why Ginetta have survived is that the Walklett brothers have been in the rare position of being almost entirely self-reliant. They could make all their own chassis, bodies, and most other components in-house, whereas the large majority of similar manufacturers sub-contracted for their major items.

The Ginetta G11, however, turned out to be something of an exception to this rule and the mere fact of reliance on an outside supplier put paid to what was potentially a money-spinner. As previously mentioned, the doors of the G11 were original steel MGB parts, and Ginetta, no matter how hard they tried, just could not get the delivery dates on these vital parts. And when they did eventually arrive — there stood a dozen left-hand doors, but no right-hand ones! Although BMC could not make doors fast enough for their own MGB, one is bound to suspect that they did not relish selling them to a manufacturer who was building a car that was reputed to be superior to their own.

Sadly, what could have been a not uncommon sight on the roads became a very rare one. Only twelve G11s were ever fully completed at the factory, and of these it is believed that six found their way to the USA.

Few Ginetta enthusiasts can have been more wrapped up with G11s than one Russell Madden of Birmingham. Russell — already the owner of a G4 Series III — had caught a glance of a G11 one day when he happened to be visiting the Witham factory. He soon learned from Bob Walklett that the G11 was no longer in production. However, the Walkletts did have one G11 body/chassis — the last left — and also some bare chassis lying around. Russell reached an agreement with Bob Walklett and purchased the lot, on the proviso that Ginetta would make new bodies, if and when Russell required them. To this day, Russell has built and sold two completed G11s and currently owns a very refined, very little used G11 which he built eighteen months ago. And he still has enough spare chassis (including a left-hand-drive one) for further projects to keep him busy over the coming years.

The Ginetta G11 sold for £1325 or £1098 in component form.

Chapter Seven

ON A PAR WITH LOTUS

Ginetta G12 (1966–1968)

THE G4 asserted its function as the backbone of the company during 1966, and was continuing its success on the race circuits when a new Ginetta made its appearance. April of that year saw the introduction of the G12. Bearing some similarity to the G4 theme, the G12 used a tubular steel spaceframe chassis with centre body/cockpit section bonded to it, and removable front and rear sections. It differed immensely, however, in its mid-engined configuration and in its role, which was to be an out-and-out racing car.

Claimed to be the first-ever British mid-engined GT car, the G12 was designed and built as a natural progression from the G4 and for entry in the Special GT class in British club racing.

The G12 was low and extremely purposeful in its styling. It had a front suspension which consisted of well-proven Triumph uprights and double wishbones (camber adjustment was provided by a rose-joint on the upper wishbone) and coil-spring/damper units. At the rear was the classic pattern of single upper transverse links with lower reversed wishbones (again with rose-joint for camber adjustment), double radius arms and coil-spring/damper units. Anti-roll bars were fitted front and rear, the latter being adjustable. Girling disc-brakes of 9½-inch diameter, emanating from the Triumph Spitfire, were fitted outboard on all four wheels. The wheels themselves were 13-inch Minilite Magnesium as a standard fitment, with the option of two widths: 6-inch or 7-inch. Dual-braking master cylinders were employed and steering was rack and pinion.

The G12 was made available in component form, selling at around £1200. Initial cars were designed to take the Cosworth 997cc SCA power unit or similar sized engines. Larger engines could be accommodated, but required extra strengthening of the chassis to take the additional power.

The Ginetta G12 was first entered in GT races by drivers such as John Burton, Chris Meek, and Willie Green. During the latter half of 1966 the 997cc SCA-engined G12 of Willie Green, a mere newcomer to racing, really was incredibly successful, and his results were to come as a real boost to the Walkletts. Green, in fact, had eleven wins — of which several were outright — from his first dozen races: a remarkable achievement, enhanced all the more by his breaking virtually every lap record in the process.

Willie Green had made his debut with the G12 on September 10 1966, at Silverstone (Peterborough Motor Club meeting) where he set a new lap record. The following day saw Green in his second race in the G12 at Snetterton, where he once again took another lap record. He also won his class and finished third overall. Other results of note that spring to mind include a race at Brands Hatch on November 27 the same year, when Green was entered in two events. In the first event he came second overall and second in his class — after starting from the back of the grid! In his other event of that day Green's 997cc G12 not only took a new lap record, but also first in class, and first overall — ahead of John Lepp in a Chevron GT and also the Barnet Motor Company 4727cc TVR Griffith driven by Gerry Marshall!

Willie Green's G12 was fitted with a 1964 Cos-

Willie Green's 997cc SCA G12

worth SCA (Formula Two) engine, to which some modifications from a later 1965 unit were added. A Hewland Mark Five gearbox with limited-slip differential was coupled to the engine, which developed around 110 bhp at about 9000 rpm. Green's first dozen or so races had been run on the narrower (6-inch x 13-inch) Minilite wheels fitted with 5.00 and 5.50 Dunlop White Spot tyres, without change.

Willie Green on his way to a clear win in a GT & Marque sports car race

Ferodo DS11 disc-pads were used in the otherwise standard braking system that used ordinary steel calipers. Fuel was housed in twin tanks, one either side of the engine compartment, driven by the same number of electric fuel-pumps to the twin-Weber downdraught carburettors. A crossflow radiator with light-alloy oil cooler attached to it, spare wheel and battery, all lived at the front of the car.

With the success of Green and others the sights were set. And it was not long before the Lotus Elans and AC Cobras were vanquished by Ginetta G12s.

Lotus had replied to the success of the Ginetta G12 with the mid-engined Europa, code-named type-47, fitted with the Lotus 165 bhp twin-cam engine. It, too, used magnesium alloy wheels all round — 8½-inch wide at the front and 10½-inch at the rear — very much wider than those used on the G12. In spite of its extra power and wider wheels, the Lotus Europa did not get the upper hand of the G12. In fact, the Europa was not terribly successful as a racing car, except when in the hands of John Miles and Jackie Oliver, both Lotus works drivers, who could occasionally beat the G12, as they did, in that order, at the Brands Hatch Boxing Day meeting in 1966. The result sheet after the race, however, placed Willie Green in second position — Jackie Oliver being given a one-minute penalty for requiring a push-start. The works Lotus 47s were fitted with temperamental Tecalamit fuel-injection which plagued them with starting problems and, on several occasions, even fires!

Internally the Ginetta G12 was somewhat sparse, but it must be remembered that it was, after all, an out-and-out racer: it still had a neatly assembled fas-

The G12s of Peter Creasey and John Burton start to slide at South Bank, before the spectacular accident depicted overleaf

The 4727cc Shelby American Cobra of Keith Hamblin ploughs into and over Paul Ridgways G12. Braking furiously, a Fiat Arbarth 1000. The silhouette is of Gerry Stream, well-known racing photographer, leaping for safety, out of the passage of another wayward G12

cia-panel, leather-rimmed steering wheel, foot-brace and well-fitting seats, albeit with no padding at the sides. The gearshift was positioned on the right side of the driver to link up with the Hewland gearbox.

Early in 1967 Willie Green had a 1594cc twin-cam engine in his G12, and at the Brands Hatch *Racing Car Show Trophy* meeting on January 22, he was again entered in two events. In the first event he came second overall, only 0.8 seconds behind the 4727cc McLaren Elva-Ford of Keith St John! Green's other event saw him finish first overall and take another lap record — ahead of a 7-litre Shelby American Cobra and a 4736cc Ford GT40!

SCA installed in a G12

Ian Tee in the G12 of Motoring News alongside a LEC Cobra driven by David Purley

During 1967 the Ginetta G12 was appearing in some numbers in GT races, of which the *Motoring News* GT Championship was probably the most attractive. Held over twenty-one rounds, this championship saw some extremely exciting racing and also a most spectacular accident which involved several G12s.

The championship was grouped into four classes: up to 1150cc, 1150cc to 1600cc, 1600cc to 2500cc and above 2500cc. Besides the 997cc-engined versions, some G12s now began to feature engines of larger capacity and as a consequence, were able to contend the various classes. Most G12s, in fact, were now running 1600cc twin-cam engines — Willie Green himself turned up at one round in a new works G12, fitted with a 172 bhp Alan Smith twin-cam engine and, although he didn't enjoy the same success that he had with his earlier SCA G12, he was still able to give the Lotus 47s and Chevrons a run for their money and managed to reap class lap records with his superb driving skill.

Willie Green's original car was now in the hands of Keith Jupp, now also featuring a twin-cam engine. Peter Creasey had installed a 2-litre Climax engine in his G12 and was getting some very promising results. Not to be outdone, *Motoring News* had a G12 of their very own entered in their championship, driven by Editor Mike Twite and co-driver Ian Tee. The Worcestershire Racing Association entered no fewer than three G12s, two Cosworth twin-

cam versions driven by John Bamford, and an SCA-engined version driven by Paul Ridgway. Another G12 exponent, John Burton, had gone to some lengths to fit a 2-litre Martin V8 engine to his car. Unfortunately it was plagued with running problems and consequently it was never the success he had hoped for. He struggled for most of the season with the engine that never gave anywhere near its reputed 200 bhp. Nearing the final rounds of the championship, Burton resorted to driving a lightweight SCA-engined G12 in which he was more successful, taking eight points in the final round of the championship by finishing a superb sixth overall in the race.

The Ginetta G12 was certainly proving its worth and had become the car to contend with. Most rounds did not, however, go without incident. Peter Creasey rolled his G12, thus requiring a total rebuild, the *Motoring News* G12 had spun off, hitting a post, hence also needing a rebuild. And further drama was afoot at round fifteen, held on August 26 at Oulton Park, when John Bamford's throttle stuck on his G12, causing the car to crash. The force was such that John was actually thrown out through the roof, amazingly without injury. And even more drama captured the scene at the penultimate round on October 8 at Brands Hatch. It happened on only the first lap when the G12s of Peter Creasey and John Burton came into contact with each other, causing both cars to spin. Taking evasive action, another G12, driven by Andy Mylius, careered off the track and into the bank; meanwhile Keith Hamblin's Shelby Cobra spectacularly collided with, and literally climbed over, the Ginetta G12 of Paul Ridgway, ripping his cockpit canopy completely off, and narrowly missing Paul himself.

The close of the championship saw G12s figure prominently in the results. G12s took four out of the first eight places in the up to 1150cc class, Paul Ridgway winning the class outright and also taking second overall in the championship in his SCA-engined G12. Seven G12s were amongst the honours in the 1150cc to 1600cc class. And the 1600cc to 2500cc class was won outright in convincing style by Peter Creasey in his 2-litre Climax-engined G12, ahead of a host of Chevrons and Porsches: no mean feat.

On the circuits the Ginetta G12 continued its onslaught into 1968, until its mantle was usurped by the emergence of the larger, more powerful, 2-litre mid-engined Chevron BMWs on very much wider wheels. The G12 was limited in its wheel-rim widths and therefore could not match these cars.

Although later versions of the G12 actually used the Lotus/Ford 1594cc twin-cam and FVA engines, and wider wheels, these never achieved the success of earlier models.

The Walkletts concluded that the arrival of the mid-engined 2-litre opposition had put paid to the competitiveness of the G12. Production was halted

Rear of Richard Dodkins G12

and it is speculated that some fifty-plus examples were built.

Shortly after its demise various attempts were made by some garages and owners to convert the G12 into a road-going car. This immensely displeased the Walkletts, who recognised all the inadequacies of such a venture, since the car had been designed specifically with the purpose of motor racing only. Their disapproval did not prevent some from trying, and one person by the name of Bruce Giddy actually had his road-going G12 featured in *Car* magazine of August 1969. He had hoped that he could build other road-going G12s for prospective customers to their individual

Brian Moody's immaculate and record-holding G12

requirements. Comment in this feature, however, showed his converted G12 to be a long way from a viable proposition as a road-car. Evidently, this did not deter others from going ahead and actually converting their cars. Even today a number of G12s are still road-registered.

As far as its racing career is concerned, the G12 is still to be seen on the circuits in Historic GT races and in hillclimbs. In recent times a well-known and popular example was the G12 owned by Richard Dodkins. Richard has competed for some years with several successes and lap records in hillclimbing and circuit racing. His G12 was instantly recognisable during the past couple of seasons with its immaculate paintwork, finished in Jaguar Heather, graced with the signature of Jimmy Saville and the Stoke Mandeville Hospital Appeal Fund, to which Richard so generously contributed.

Other drivers have had successes in recent years in their G12s, but perhaps a special mention should be made of the G12 owned and raced by Brian Moody who lives in Jersey. Brian's G12 can only be described as an absolutely superb example. Brian bought the car in 1974 for use in sprints and hill-

Walter Flükiger's famous G12 'Spyder' in Switzerland

climbs in Jersey. It was raced in English hillclimbs on a couple of occasions when Brian loaned the car to Chris Tufnell. In 1980 Brian became the record holder on Bouley Bay with a time of 50.55 seconds in the GT and Modsports section up to 1600cc. He held this record for some two years before loosing it in July 1982. Nonetheless, he is hoping to regain it again during Easter 1983. His car is powered by a Lotus/Ford twin-cam 1558cc engine with Hewland gearbox.

A number of G12s managed to find their way out of this country: two were raced in Switzerland, probably the most notable one being owned by Walter Flückiger, who was twice Swiss Hillclimb Champion in the Sportscars up to 1-litre category. The first occasion was in 1968 when Walter's G12 was as original. During the months preceding the next season new regulations were introduced. Amongst these was a change in the rules in the category Walter raced in — his G12 was now ineligible as only open cars were allowed in the class. Walter Flückiger took the most drastic action by having the roof of his G12 literally cut off, and the body vastly modified. From this his G12 'Spyder' evolved and it looked as elegant as ever, and proved to be as reliable — Walter took the championship for the second time. Sadly, this car was eventually broken up and sold for scrap.

Another G12 of note was the one owned from new by Ginetta's US importer, Art Allen. Recently advertised for sale, this has been the only G12 ever to have been raced in the USA.

*Superb road-
converted G12 of
Austrian, Armin
Eigelsreiter*

*G12 at the 1966
Racing Car Show*

The Ultimate road-going G12

One Ginetta G12 that cannot go without mention, is another that found its way to the USA. This example, however, was turned into the ultimate road machine. Although the Walkletts were said to be against the G12 being turned into a road car, there is some evidence that they may have more than pondered the idea, as some of the last chassis made were fitted with mounting points to take an Imp power unit — and apparently one G12 was actually fitted with an Imp transaxle. The following is how one professional designer pursued the task and succeeded.

Richard A. Petit became head of the Advanced Vehicle Concepts studio at the Ford Design Center in Dearborn, USA, because he is a complete automobile design enthusiast and a doer.

In 1962 he decided he was going to build a special GT/road/racing car, being motivated (in his own words) "by my desire to own and operate a specialized vehicle of that nature, since I am always striving for the 'unique identity' as a designer and possessed with a competition-orientated ego." By April of 1966 the plan of approach was sufficiently in mind for him to discuss its potential with Dr

Wilfred C Becker, Director of Wayne State University's Industrial Design Department in Detroit. It was agreed that Petit would pursue his Master of Arts degree, specialising in Industrial Design, and using the design study and construction report on the car as his thesis.

Providentially, the Ford Motor Company sent him to its Design Center in England for a year at this point which gave him a fine chance to research the proprietary power train and chassis component that he would need. After deliberation he chose Ginetta Cars Ltd and purchased a G12 steel-tube space-frame chassis from their West End Works, Witham in Essex, this featuring full-independent suspension, Girling disc-brakes, rack-and-pinion steering, and a championship competition heritage. The specially modified engine sits amidships and operates through a Hewland 4-speed gearbox.

The original G12 body design was refined in sketches, precisely developed in a quarter-size clay form, and then twice duplicated in fiberglass — one shell for a show model and the other used as a dimensional guide for a full-scale model.

Petit (now back in Dearborn, USA) was most fortunate in being able to enlist the help of his cousin, David Conley, who at the time was a member of the Ford Motor Design Center clay modelling staff. Together and in a totally professional style they constructed a surface plate, buck form, templates, and accurate registration devices for a full-scale clay

Ultra-smooth — note how doors run into roof line

The photographs on these pages show just what a beautiful machine Petit's G12 is

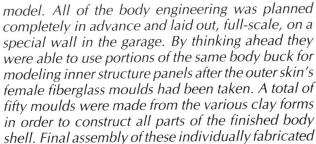

model. All of the body engineering was planned completely in advance and laid out, full-scale, on a special wall in the garage. By thinking ahead they were able to use portions of the same body buck for modeling inner structure panels after the outer skin's female fiberglass moulds had been taken. A total of fifty moulds were made from the various clay forms in order to construct all parts of the finished body shell. Final assembly of these individually fabricated panels, however, required only a bare minimum of trimming for a perfect fit.

The interior specifications reflect that the car is a full road machine and not just a show shell or racing exercise. Minimum instrumentation, toggle switches, and semi-reclining seats are carefully placed while other features include a collapsible steering column, padded steering wheel, fire extinguisher, glove tray, and full seat belt harness combination with concealed attachment points. Additional items are the foam-filled and explosion-proof fuel tanks, an emergency flasher system, electric side marker lights, windshield defroster, washer, and a 3-speed special heavy-duty wiper system.

The thing that really sets Petit's G12 apart is the handsome and painstaking thoroughness of its planning in every detail followed by the absolutely faultless craftsmanship of its execution. Truthfully, it is a masterful work — a delight to the observer, operator, and a tribute to the designer's perseverance and skill.

Reprinted, in part, with the very kind permission of *Road & Track* USA.

It is a fitting tribute also, that Petit chose Ginetta in pursuit of his ideal and ultimate automobile.

One point that is not mentioned in the *Road & Track* extract is that the Walkletts made special alterations to Petit's G12 chassis in order to accommodate his taller-than-average height.

Richard Petit still works today for the Ford Design Centre in Dearborn, USA, and continues to hold his affection for the Ginetta marque. He still has in his possession, and treasures, the ¼-scale glassfibre model, finished in bright red, of the final car — which, incidentally, had a much less raked screen and was smoother looking than the model.

At the time when Petit and his cousin had completed the car, the Walkletts had considered acquiring the moulds from Petit as a package to produce their own very special road-going car, using a 3-litre engine and ZF gearbox. However, since Richard Petit was so tied up in his job at the Ford Design Centre, and consequently was obliged to spend a year living in Italy — and with the Walkletts' own very busy programme (plus the fact that they found the cost of the ZF gearbox prohibitive) — the project never materialised.

This car would have been the so-called G20 road car.

Chapter Eight

THE BEST SELLER

Ginetta G15 (1968–1974) incorporating G13 and G14

WITH the G12 no longer competitive in racing, once again the Walklett brothers were poised to announce another new Ginetta. On this occasion the painstaking and deliberate planning was to yield their most successful model to date. Development had continued behind the scenes whilst the centre of attention had been focused on the other Ginetta models, the G10 and G11, the G12 and, of course, the evergreen G4.

Designer Ivor Walklett initially planned a road-going 2-seater coupé, using a backbone chassis and a conventional mechanical layout, with the body a sort of scaled-down version of the G11. One chassis was, in fact, completed but regrettably the car, which would have received the designation G14, never got beyond the chassis stage and consequently was shelved. The Walkletts had preference for a chassis that extended fully to the outside sills. Incidentally the leap from G12 to G14 was

purely because of superstitions associated with the number 13, and for this reason no number 13 was designated.

Without delay a new development programme had taken over. Again it was a similar plan for a road-going 2-seater sports coupé, but this time looking towards a more sophisticated approach. Early in 1967 a new chassis and body had been designed with the intention of accepting a rear-engined set-up. One requirement of this new car was that it should feature a smallish power-unit, in order to keep insurance at a reasonable level: it was decided that the solution must lie in Rootes' Hillman Imp. The Imp had been introduced by Rootes in 1963, its all-alloy 875cc engine, derived from the famous Coventry Climax power-unit, producing 42 bhp at 5000 rpm. However, it was not long before Rootes launched their Sunbeam derivative, the Imp Sport, which produced 55 bhp at 6100 rpm. The increase

An example of an
early type G15
owned by Kay
Williams for many
years

in power had been obtained by the addition of a
redesigned cylinder head, and high-lift camshaft
coupled to twin Stromberg carburettors.

This was the answer to the Walkletts' prayers.
Contact was quickly made with Rootes, who were
only too pleased to supply engines and components
and in no time at all a deal had been struck. Choosing the Imp engine struck an old note, when it is
remembered that at one stage the Ginetta G4 was to
have been powered by a production version of
Climax's famous 'fire-pump' motor.

The brothers had recently joined SMMT (the So-
ciety of Motor Manufacturers and Traders), and this
gave the Walkletts the privilege to exhibit at the
annual Earls Court Motor Show. Wasting no time at
all and only one year after the launch of the Sunbeam Imp Sport, Ginetta launched the G15 in prototype form in the company's first appearance at the
London Motor Show in 1967. Its debut aroused
enormous interest and its price of only £799, in
component form, made it very attractive. The
Ginetta G15 was, indeed, to sell more profusely
than any other Ginetta model to date and has
become the best known, if not the most popular, of
the marque.

Production of the G15 did not commence until
August of the following year, however, during
which time the cost had risen to £849, entirely
because of the huge price increase of bought-in
components. The first production G15s, of which

only a handful were built, had the radiator at the
rear of the car in conventional Imp fashion, but this
was soon changed because of the dubious cooling
in this position; and considering that Ginetta nearly
always end up with their cars being raced, it seemed
judicious to resite the radiator at the sharp end. All
further production G15s consequently had their
radiators positioned thus.

These early G15s, known as the Series I, had a
simple recirculatory heater, windscreen washers,
and unusual sun-visors which were attached to the
tops of the door frames, but surprisingly these —
normally regarded as standard items — were all
listed as optional extras! Other options included a
sunroof, wide alloy wheels and radial tyres. The
Series I G15 had only 4-inch-wide steel rims with

skinny crossply tyres, but surprisingly this was no detriment to the handling and roadholding — which could only be described as astonishing.

The Series II G15 very quickly followed on the heels of the Series I and, for the reason already mentioned, this also had the radiator positioned at the front of the car. The glassfibre fascia panel was redesigned and looked smart in its black textured finish, and new, better seats were fitted.

In 1971 the Series III model of the G15 appeared, with further changes and improvements. The obvious external alteration was to the rear side-screens. These had been enlarged to increase all-round visibility and were more complementary to the shape of the car. The door screens were of a sliding type and used locking catches identical to those fitted to early Minis. With no window-winding mechanism necessary extra space was created and this was conveniently used for making large door pockets. The radiator nose-cone, previously detachable, was now an integral part of the front body section. The front bumper, comprising two halves of a Volkswagen Beetle bumper, was now made to look much neater with a moulded section between the two halves instead of just butting together. The rear bumper originated from the BMC Riley Elf. Other changes included the previously recessed front indicator lamps now fitted flush, and the conventional screw-on fuel-filler cap replaced by a large magnetic flip-up type. One optional extra was a Wood-Jeffreys electric cooling fan fitted in front of the radiator. It was thermostatically controlled by a sensor fitted near the thermostat housing, or independently from a switch on the fascia panel.

Inside the car, the heater (still an option) was of a more efficient type from the Triumph GT6. The windscreen wiper motor was moved from its original position under the dash on the passenger side, to a similar position on the driver's side. Also re-sited was the screen-wash bottle, originally positioned in the front compartment, now inside near the driver's wheel arch: although this prevented the screen-wash from freezing in icy weather, it looked rather unsightly. Most owners relocated the container to its original position.

Throughout the production of the Series III G15, further detail changes became evident. These included the addition of a steering/ignition lock, a non-magnetic flip-up fuel-filler cap, a change in brake discs and size of pads, and differences in the front and rear dampers fitted. Rear dampers were now as those used on the Imp. Earlier G15s had had dampers with a top mounting that was secured inside the car underneath the two cones on the rear parcel shelf. The front dampers, originally Imp, were replaced by units with a higher spring-mounting seat and at the same time the top suspension wishbone mounting points were lowered. Alloy wheels (an optional extra) were Mk 1 Cosmic, made specially for the G15.

*Teabreak at
Sudbury! —
G15 production
line*

66

With their business literally booming there was no doubt that the tiny G15 had really taken off for the Walkletts. In fact, orders were now coming in thick and fast and the brothers were finding their Witham premises to be a little on the cramped side. Already in mind there were plans for another new model, so it was decided that the time had arrived for expansion. Plans were immediately put under way and by March 1972, Ginetta Cars Limited were housed in a new, spacious, and purpose-built factory at Sudbury in Suffolk: 40,000 square feet on a 3½ acre site and with enough room for further expansion if required. The new premises were fully equipped with two large paint-spray booths, both with low-bake ovens, separate glassfibre and laying-up areas and, of course, the much needed and essential production-line facilities. The G15 chassis was made on site, fabricated on an extremely substantial master-jig using square-section steel tube and sheet. To enable the company to cope with the increased demand, the workforce was increased to some fifty employees and output was raised simultaneously.

Inevitably, the Walkletts found that their new factory proved to be more costly to run than their previous smaller Witham premises but nonetheless the order book continued to fill, and rapidly too. Between four and six G15s were now rolling off the production line at the end of each week.

At this point we come to the one area in which Ginetta, as a company, have differed greatly in comparison to other production car makers: that of a dealership network. Rather they would sell direct—inviting each potential customer to the factory so that he could see just how the product is built and

The rear of a late G15 and how engine access is made so simple

exactly what he would be buying. This procedure resulted in extremely friendly relationships between the customers and the factory. This kind of approach to selling their product meant, however, that the factory was at times swamped with visitors and potential customers, and proved to be very time-consuming. Eventually it made the brothers concede that the point had been reached where it was time to branch out; and in no time at all a small dealer network had been set up to cope with the ever-creasing sales.

Late in 1972 more cosmetic changes appeared on the Ginetta G15. The front indicators were now housed in small forward mounting pods and special ratchet-type door stops replaced the previous, and rather poor, method which had relied upon a piece of wire to restrain the door. In fact if a door was

continually allowed to swing open the wire would inevitably snap. Sidelights became incorporated in the headlights, the petrol tank was now made of steel, as opposed to glassfibre, thus complying with recently introduced new safety regulations — albeit with a reduced capacity (earlier tanks having had a capacity of some 5½ gallons, the new tanks held approximately one gallon less). Redesigned interior door trim panels, updated with new flush-fitting interior and exterior door handles taken from the Austin/Morris Marina range, were fitted.

This model was predominantly sold in component form. Everything continued to look promising for the Walklett brothers and their G15 — until April 1st 1973. This was the date which saw the introduction of the dreaded Value Added Tax. This increased the selling price of a G15 dramatically to £1395.

Neat fascia of a late type G15

Interior of a late type G15 showing the grand-prix seating position

VAT had the effect of virtually killing all component cars. All G15s produced from April 1st were in fully-built form only. In the hope of keeping sales to earlier levels, promotion was increased and the Series IV G15 was launched. Appearing in advertisements in the motoring media under the heading of 'Ginetta move into top-gear for 1973' this G15 featured Mark 2 Cosmic alloy wheels and radial tyres as standard fitment, plus many other extras. The sales push did not have the desired effect, however, and sadly this eventually led to production of the G15 being halted — just one year later in April 1974. Although sales were diminishing due to VAT, it was the oil price increases and also further imminent cost increases that really put paid to the G15.

At its demise more than 800 of the Ginetta G15 had been built.

The Ginetta G15 was of diminutive proportions, although not exaggeratedly so by any means. The amount of room inside the car was most surprising for such a small vehicle. In fact, such was its size that it looked to be dwarfed even by a Mini. Despite its size, its ingenious styling made it a most attractive model, with smooth flowing lines that today belie its years. It is cleverly designed so that it appears to be front-engined when in fact it is, of course, rear-engined. Setting aside its many attributes — economy, performance, safety, to name but a few — it can only be described as a design of excellence: especially so when one considers the inconceivable amounts of money that large motor manufacturers spend trying to achieve performance and economy as a combined package. With very little in the way of resources, but a great deal of combined talent, the Walkletts had produced a sports car that was so economical that it could return a genuine 50 mpg, yet at the same time it could accelerate to 50 mph in 8.9 seconds and reach a top speed of 100 mph — all with an engine of only 875cc! And when it came to its roadholding and cornering ability, this could only be described by using superlatives! It was virtually in a class of its own. Its safety aspect was also excellent, with its full-length hefty steel chassis, not only a front but also a rear laminated screen, and a collapsible steering column. A G15'S' model was also available; it used a larger capacity 998cc Imp engine and was capable of propelling the car from 0-60 mph in 9 seconds, and had a top speed of 115 mph.

The G15 was a well-made, strong sports car, with its pretty glassfibre body bolted to the full-length steel chassis — and not bonded, as stated in some past literature on the model.

Although a large number of G15s were sold in component form, or 'kit-car' to use the loosely phrased term, the amount of work involved in putting together a G15 was minimal. In fact, a car could be completed quite easily in one weekend. The G15 came virtually complete; with all doors, bonnet, boot, screens, seats, carpet, trim, instruments etc,

already fitted and the glassfibre body painted in the colour of the customer's choice.

The rear suspension of the G15 was derived from the Hillman Imp, whereas the front suspension was basically Triumph Spitfire with a Ginetta-designed anti-roll bar added. The suspension was all-independent, combining coil spring/telescopic damper units at the front and separate coil springs and telescopic dampers at the rear. Braking was in the form of 9-inch-diameter Triumph Spitfire discs at the front and 8-inch- diameter drums at the rear. Steering was rack and pinion from the Triumph Spitfire with the actual column originating from the Hillman Imp and the two items linked by a Ginetta design of two Torrington universal joints.

The interior of the G15 was pleasantly finished to a high standard using a top-quality grey cloth trim for the headlining, and high quality wall-to-wall carpeting with leathercloth-bound edging. Seats were of a fixed recline shape, designed by Ginetta, giving a 'grand-prix' driving position with excellent lateral support. The seat frames were also made by Ginetta, with the seat covering in a black leathercloth undertaken by a local trimmer. Finally, a real-leather-rimmed, alloy-spoked, steering wheel was fitted to complement the interior.

Luggage space was confined mainly to the inside of the G15. The front bonnet, despite its appearance, hid only the fuel tank, hydraulics and spare wheel — leaving little room for anything more than a handful of tools. Nonetheless, for a sports car — and in this case a very small sports car — room inside the car, especially behind the seats, was surprisingly generous. This would amply take a couple reasonably-sized suitcases, albeit after a struggle to lift them over the fixed-back seats. Beyond this space there was a large parcel shelf with a ledge and, of course, both doors had large pockets in which to stow any other items.

Entry into and exit from the G15 was not as difficult as its diminutive size suggested. Someone on the large size would probably have found things a little cramped because of the narrowness of the seats, but otherwise leg- and head-room was ample for all, even the tallest drivers.

When it came to engine maintenance and accessibility , the Ginetta G15 was second to none. The complete rear-section of the car hinged upwards, once two catches had been released by a special T-piece key that was stowed in the car. The engine and transaxle could be removed together in very little time, thus simplifying any major operations.

In the competitive arena the Ginetta G15 has, to this day, been outstandingly successful: so successful, in fact, that a couple of seasons or so back some very controversial decisions were taken by the British Racing Drivers' Club (BRDC) and the British Racing and Sports Car Club (BRSCC). These decisions made it impossible for the tiny G15 to enter further Production Sports Car races organised by these two major clubs. These open-to-question decisions gave rise to much correspondence in the motoring press, but to no avail. The decisions stood and one has to suspect that the G15 was becoming an embarrassment to the BRDC & BRSCC hierarchy: a case of the G15 being too successful? It certainly seemed to have been that way when one considers that the previous (1980) season had seen a somewhat arbitrary grouping in this same competition that put the tiny 998cc-engined Ginetta into the same class as cars like 1600cc TVRs and 2-litre TR7s. This, it seemed, was not enough and the BRDC/BRSCC then allowed a 2300cc-engined Panther Lima to compete in the same class! Much to the delight of Ginetta enthusiasts and the factory staff, ploys like this were unable to halt the success of the tiny Ginetta. It had won the championship outright in 1979, and then came second in class the following season: these successes proved that it would take some beating. Finally, it was only the sad plight of its arbitrary exclusion that could curtail its success.

Its ineligibility to compete in this race series overlooked the fact that the G15 had been an integral part of the Production Sports Car scene: thus its exclusion dramatically reduced the variety and spectacle of this form of racing. The small-engined and diminutive Ginetta G15 was constantly up amongst the front-runners, playing havoc with the much more expensive, larger-engined machinery — TR7s, E-type Jaguars and so on. There is no doubt that the omission of the attractive Ginetta G15 has made the BRDC/BRSCC-organised series very much less exciting.

Fortunately, all was not lost. Other motor racing clubs, such as the 750 Motor Club, organise events in which the G15 is still able to participate and Donington has its own series for Production GTs in which the G15 is eligible. Although obviously not appearing in the same numbers, a small contingent of G15s has raced on the circuits during the 1982 season: probably the most successful driver being Roger Bowden, who, in fact, was only just pipped in the final round of the Garelli championship for road-going sports cars. 1982 also saw the revival of the Four-Hour Relay Race, held at Oulton Park circuit, and this event was won on handicap by

Team Ginetta. Three of the four Ginettas taking part were G15s — an excellent achievement. It is of note that whereas in recent times most racing cars are trailered to and from an event, the G15s can still be seen being driven to the circuit by their owners, raced on the circuit, then driven home again. It is that kind of vehicle.

Initially, the Ginetta G15 first appeared in motor sport in a Modsports guise. The most successful Ginetta drivers in this form of racing were undoubtedly Barry Wood and Alison Davis. It was the mod-ified G15 of Alison Davis, built by her husband Roger and brother-in-law Chris, which originally appeared on the circuits in 1971. It made immediate and dramatic impact by achieving several victories in the smaller capacity classes. The car went extremely well and was immaculately turned out, its clean white paintwork delicately covered with sponsorship from Femfresh Deodorants. It became a very popular car on the circuits and received an accolade as one of the best-prepared racing cars.

It was in June of the same year that the Walkletts

Alison Davis coming into Woodcote, at Silverstone 1971 ahead of overall winner John Harper in his E-type

themselves entered a 'works' Modsports G15, driven by Barry Wood, and this car also gave the opposition plenty to think about. By the close of the season, Wood had amassed a total of eleven class wins, two 2nd in class and one 2nd overall in only fifteen outings. In the meanwhile, Alison Davis continued with her success in the G15 and became the British Women Racing Drivers' Champion.

The most memorable race in the Modsports series during that 1971 season occurred when these two drivers came up against one another and battled it out on the Grand Prix circuit of Brands Hatch. Barry Wood, in the works car, eventually succumbed to the G15 of Alison Davis.

Whilst Barry Wood continued to be the works driver for some seasons to come, Alison sold her car because of a seriously limited budget. It is ironic then that some ten years later, in 1982, the old 'Femfresh' G15 has ended up with, and is raced by, none other than Barry Wood himself.

Besides circuit racing, the Ginetta G15 was also highly successful in sprinting — notably in the hands of Brian Tavender, who, in the early 1970s, was the acknowledged king of the Silverstone sprint championship.

It was during the seasons of 1976 and 1977 that another name came onto the circuit scene — David Beams. He and his team-mate, Garry Taylor, had been Ginetta enthusiasts for some years — together they had run the Ginetta Owners' Club in the early 1970s, until it was disbanded in 1975, and they had competed in smaller events such as sprints and production car trials. Their first attempt at the latter resulted in their winning! During 1974 David Beams

Alison at Thruxton, 1972, in front of John Pearson's Jaguar XK120

Barry Wood, cornering hard in the works G15

Alison Davis's 'Femfresh' G15, now much modified, leading a Sprite, Turner and Marcos GT during 1972 at Brands Hatch. Alison came 1st in class

Alison's award-winning G15

Barry Wood again in the works G15

won the CSAN Trophy in his G15 for the highest placed road-going car at the Valance hillclimb. Moreover, Beams had the pleasure of retaining this trophy the following year in 1975, when he also became the BARC Sprint/Hillclimb Champion.

With appetite whetted, David Beams decided to try his hand at bigger things. On a very limited budget and with the aid of team-mate Garry Taylor and friends, Beams's Ginetta G15 was completely stripped and rebuilt to enable them to enter Production Sports Car Racing (Prodsports). To be eligible for this category of motor racing the cars had to be in a basically road-going form. No modifications to the suspension or engine were allowed. This was the great virtue of the G15 — it could be used as everyday transport and yet was competitive enough

to be used in club racing with very little or no alteration.

March 1976 saw David Beams in his first attempt at circuit racing at Snetterton. After an excellent practice session he had earned a place on the third row of the grid. The actual race got under way and Beams drove the little G15 superbly, certainly surprising the opposition. Unfortunately, on the last lap, Beams was forced to withdraw when still lying third in class. The bright red G15 had developed a misfire causing a loss of power. Back in the pits the cause was traced to an air-cleaner bolt which had worked loose, allowing the air-cleaner element to slip down and partially obstruct the flow of air to one carburettor. There was some consolation for

Beams, however, as he had established the fastest lap in his class — and in only his first circuit race.

As the season progressed, so Beams improved with his driving and at the close of the season he had finished 2nd in class. He also held the lap records at Ingliston, Brands Hatch and Mallory Park — the latter on both the long and short circuits.

At the beginning of the 1977 season Beams's G15 appeared, newly resprayed in gleaming white, and this time with more sponsorship. Driving superbly throughout, in what was to be his best season of racing, he clinched not only the winner in class in the Silverstone Production Sports Car Championship, but he also won outright the 'Certina Swiss Watches Production Sports Car Championship'. Beams in his G15 had made further lap records at Brands Hatch, Silverstone, Mallory Park (long circuit), Snetterton, Oulton Park and Donington.

Throughout the season, Beams's G15 had brought much excitement. Possibly the most memorable moments came during a dice with the 5.3-litre V12 E-type Jaguar of Martin Birrane, the ex-Le Man's competitor, at Brands Hatch. For close on five laps Beams and Birrane had battled it out, the more powerful Jaguar gaining enormously on the G15 down the straights, but unable to capitalise thanks to the phenomenal cornering power of the G15. The spectators were all on tenderhooks with this spectacle, but were most amused when the mighty V12 Jaguar spun off at Paddock in its vain

76

attempt to keep up with the diminutive Ginetta G15.

Production Sports Car Racing was to see more and more G15s appear the following season. David Beams had sold his highly successful G15 to Steve Cole, who took the lap record at Thruxton and continued successfully to win his class in the Lucas/CAV Production Sports Car Championship during 1978.

1978 also saw another competitive area where the G15 was establishing itself — Production Car Trials. Keith Jones and his wife, Ann, are real enthusiasts; both participate in Production Car Trials in Wales. In 1978 Keith became the Welsh Production Car Trials champion, and during 1981 he not only won class six in the BTRDA Production Car Trials, but also won, outright, the Glyn Edwards Championship. The latter championship is run by the four North Wales motor clubs, and consists of twelve events: four PCTs, four autotests (two on tarmac and two on grass), and four rallies (two stage and two road events). Keith competed in ten out of the twelve events — nine in his G15, which only goes to show its versatility, to win a championship that had attracted over one hundred and fifty competitors in a vast array of powerful machinery.

The 1979 season saw the return of Alison Davis to racing a Ginetta G15, this time in the Prodsports guise. A second-hand road-going G15 had been purchased, was completely rebuilt, once again by husband Roger, and brother-in-law, Chris, and entered in the appropriate series. Immaculately pre-

Keith Jones, G15 trials expert, on his way to a trophy

David and the Goliaths! David Beams tiny G15 amongst the larger, more expensive prodsports machinery

The author's modified road-going G15

pared and very distinctive in its signal yellow paintwork, Alison took her G15 to a convincing out-right victory in the DB Motors/Cars and Car Conversions Championship. This achievement also gained Alison the very distinguished title of Britain's first-ever Lady National Race Champion. Alison's G15 had completed eighteen out of a total of nineteen races, having to retire on just the one occasion — and that was due to a broken fanbelt! And all of the eighteen finishes were either 1sts or 2nds, breaking the Silverstone lap record in the process, previously held by David Beams: all in all, an incredible achievement.

It was the 1980 season that saw the beginning of the end for the Ginetta G15 in the BRDC/BRSCC organised Prodsports events. The new regulations, as already mentioned, had allowed in the 2.3-litre Panther Lima, formidable opposition to say the least, in the same class as the G15. This ridiculous and grossly unfair treatment was followed, during the next season of 1981, by the new ruling which was, in effect, a ban on the G15 from these races. Fortunately, no matter what happens in the future, the G15 has a superb competition history and *no one* can take that away.

Overall 1979 prodsports champion, Alison Davis, entering Woodcote in her immaculate G15, ahead of a Europa and TR7

Roger Bowden's G15 came within a whisper of winning the Garelli road-going sports car championship in 1982

Andy Woolley, a true racing enthusiast who actually drives his G15 to the circuits to race

Californian G15s

During 1978, an American by the name of Art Allen — who had previously dealt with the Walkletts in the capacity of a Ginetta US agent, and had purchased G12 and G16 models — commissioned the brothers to build him some very special G15s, after being inspired by the success on the racing circuits of David Beams's example.

Art Allen wanted the G15 body to be cosmetically updated and alterations to be made to the chassis to accommodate a different power unit, with the intention of selling the new cars in the USA. The Walkletts discussed the project put to them and decided to take it on. Serious thought had to be given to the layout of the new chassis, and this

Art Allen posing with one of his G15 Super S.

81

resulted in a slightly heavier frame than original, designed to accept post-1969 Volkswagen engines and transaxles. The steering would, of course, have to be adapted for left-hand drive, and a new mould would have to be made for the dashboard to accommodate the instruments on the left-hand side.

A new G15 glassfibre body was made, complete with wide wheel arches. At the front of the car a new combined bumper/air dam unit was bolted on, whilst at the rear a new deep wrap-round bumper was fitted, complete with recesses for fitment of

G15 Super S

either fog or reversing lights. Access to the Volkswagen engine was by a boot lid finishing along the body line, rather than the traditional hinged complete rear end section. The fuel tank was housed in its normal position, but the filler cap did not protrude through the bonnet in usual G15 style — instead it was hidden under a flush bonnet. The interior was very smart, fully carpeted and fitted with reclining seats finished in a cloth fabric. Finally, setting the car off, were wide 6-inch x 13-inch alloy wheels and emblazoned along the sides of the car, in large lettering, was the name 'Ginetta' with accompanying stripes. The car also had all the necessary safety features to meet the Californian Highway Patrol road requirements. A second of these special G15s, incidentally designated G15 Super S, was built and both cars were shipped to the USA.

In California, Art Allen had literature printed with the aim of getting orders for this new derivative of the G15. In the event, the G15 Super S was not a very successful venture, due in part possibly to the 60–90-day delivery date. However, although this derivative of the G15 had been developed for export only, G15 owners were allowed to benefit from some of the development by being able to purchase the front combined bumper/air dam, wheel arches and rear bumper. In fact, many G15 owners have now fitted some of these additions to their cars.

Chapter Nine

BELATED SUCCESS

Ginetta G16 (1968–1969)

THE Ginetta G16, another out and out racing car, was really a continuation of the G12 theme, but it looked somewhat larger and more aggressive. Intended as a means of levelling the score with the Chevron GTs, the G16 was a 2-litre GT designed to be able to accept a variety of power units.

Although it followed the pattern of the earlier G12, it was built as an open-top car to conform with new Group 6 racing regulations which had been introduced in 1968. This would also allow it to compete in international sports car races. Like the G12, and the earlier G4, it too had removable front and rear body sections, and the usual full-length, very rigid, steel chassis.

The first Ginetta G16s made their appearances on the circuits midway into the 1968 racing calendar. They were run by the Worcestershire Racing Association, in the hands of two drivers — John Burton and John Bamford. Because the Worcestershire Racing Association was in full control of these cars, the progress of development was, predictably, less satisfactory than it could have been on the model; but at the same time the Walkletts were far too preoccupied with other projects, including the introduction of the G15.

The G16s driven by John Burton and John Bamford for the Worcestershire Racing Association were not very successful, even though they competed in a number of events. John Bamford's G16 was, on occasion, fitted with a BMW 1991cc engine. Other engines that were used in G16s were Ford, Coventry Climax and BRM. One G16, prepared by Brian Alexander, was fitted with an ex-BMC Oldsmobile power unit, one of the many from which the Rover V8 engine was developed.

Although by the close of the 1968 season the Ginetta G16 had not achieved the hoped-for success, nonetheless some privately entered examples

*Worcestershire
Racing Association
driver, John
Bamford, in his
BMW-engined
G16, closely
followed by
a GT40, at
Crystal Palace,
October 1968*

84

did gain the odd creditable result, notably Jeremy Richardson's G16, which was fitted with a powerful 1975cc Coventry Climax engine, and S N Moffet's FVA-engined example raced in Ireland.

The Walklett brothers tried to remedy the situation with some changes and development on the G16 before the following, 1969, season of racing. A small screen replaced the fuller screen which had used a T-bar header rail arrangement. This gave the G16 a much lower overall frontal area. An interesting and attractive fairing was added, built onto the

body above the fascia panel and returned round the tops of both doors to line up with the step on the rear bonnet. Other changes included the fitment of wider Minilite alloy wheels, stronger driveshafts, and different spring ratings.

Coinciding with this development on the car, the Walkletts decided to build a works version designated the G16A, and this was fitted with a brand new, very powerful, 2-litre BRM V8 engine. This works G16A was driven, on one occasion, by Ian Tee. The Walkletts allowed him a drive whilst his

G16 on front row of the grid

John Bamford at speed in the 1968 Silverstone Martini International Trophy race

Remains of Ian Tee's crashed G16 at Snetterton

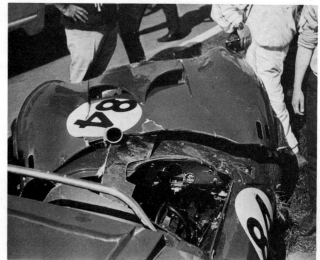

own G16A BRM was at the Witham factory undergoing repairs after a frustrating accident that Ian had been involved in at Snetterton. Encouraged by achieving the fastest lap, and leading on every lap, Ian was unfortunately put out of the race when his G16 was nudged at Russell Corner by a Chevron B8, forcing him to crash the G16.

With Bev Bond at the wheel, the works BRM V8 G16A did gain some success, however, on the local Snetterton circuit, but overall it did not obtain anything like the results that had been hoped for. Inevitably, therefore, the G16 was dropped after only a couple of seasons of racing.

*Ian Tee in the
works G16 flanked
by the enthusiastic
Walklett brothers*

Surprisingly, most of the eight G16s that were built are still extant today: one exception, though, is chassis number 001. This was purchased new by Art Allen who raced the car in the USA, powered by a Coventry Climax engine. Unfortunately it was involved in a heavy crash at Monterey and totally destroyed. Jeremy Richardson's G16 was another that was involved in a crash abroad. It is reported that at Mugello race circuit in Italy, his G16 decided to make a spectacular leap into one of the considerable voids at the sides of this somewhat alarming circuit. Fortunately for Mr Richardson there were some trees on this Italian hillside not far from the track, and it was upon these that the G16 landed, upside down. The driver's life was saved by his harness which held him securely in the car!

Ian Tee's G16A cornering hard— followed by a Chevron GT

Well-known Cobra and Porsche driver, Gerry Tyack, in his record-breaking G16

89

Peter Cook's G16 with rear body removed

An immaculate G16—one of two owned by Peter Cook

Success was to come for some G16s, however, on the hills and in sprints. John Bamford's G16 was purchased by the well-known Cobra and Porsche driver, Gerry Tyack, whose Curfew Garage, at Moreton-in-Marsh, Glos, is littered with its owner's racing achievements. The RAC Motor Sport Yearbook of 1971 lists him as National Record holder driving his FVA-engined G16 in the 1500–2000cc class, held at Elvington on the 12th July 1970. From flying starts in the 500 metres and 1 kilometre races, he achieved record times of 7.79 seconds (143.48 mph) and 15.45 seconds (144.36 mph) respectively. Today the G16 sits in the showroom of his garage, and Mr Tyack reminisces that on no occasion can he remember the G16 failing to gain a class win in any of the events he entered, which were numerous.

Of the other G16s remaining today one resides in Norfolk, one in Leicestershire, another is in Cambridgeshire — apparently being turned into a road car; Ginetta's works G16A remains at the Witham factory; and Peter Cook of Derby, has two — one undergoing restoration, whilst the other is used in hillclimbing events. The latter has gained some success in Peter's competent hands, currently holding the 'Classic' car class records on all three hills in the Midlands Hillclimb Championship. This leaves only one G16 whose present whereabouts is unknown.

91

John Bamford's G16 on the outside

Side shot of Ian Tee in his G16

Chapter Ten

THE FORMULA DREAM

Ginetta G17 (1969–1970) incorporating G18, G19, G20

LATE in 1968, a very busy period for the Ginetta company, the Walkletts embarked upon a programme of single-seater Formula racing cars. Not forgetting the problems they had encountered with the G8, previously the only single-seater built by the company, the first of these new single-seaters, the Ginetta G17, used a simple straightforward space-frame chassis made of round and square steel tube, with conventional, all-independent, suspension of wishbones and combined coil spring/damper units. Wide 13-inch Minilite magnesium alloy wheels were supplied as standard. The glassfibre body was made in three sections — the main cockpit section extended from the line of a steel roll-over hoop to the front of the chassis frame. This section was recessed along its whole length, on either side, to facilitate simple location and easy removal of the long sleek nose cone. The final section fitted behind the driver/cockpit and covered the power unit. A small perspex screen was also fitted. The power unit employed in the G17 was the 998cc Imp engine and transaxle.

The Walkletts received a number of enquiries for the G17, and also for the G18 which they introduced at the same time. This was a single-seater virtually identical with the G17, but intended for racing in Formula Ford 1600. It was fitted with a Ford engine, steel wheels and road tyres. Because there were so very few differences between the two cars, a driver could enter either a Formula Four or a Formula Ford event simply by substitution of the wheels, the tyres, and the power unit.

With these two cars in production, the Walkletts set to work on the next cars on their programme; a Formula Three single-seater, the G19, and even a prestigious Formula One car, the G20. The latter had for some time been the brothers' ambition. Their original plan was to build this during the

*Peter Voigt,
anxiously awaiting
the start of his first
event in the G17, at
Brunton, in
April 1970*

winter months of 1968–69, using a BRM 3-litre V12 engine. Unfortunately, pressure of work obliged them to postpone this long-cherished ambitious Formula One project for a further twelve months; and ultimately a combination of adverse factors compelled them to abandon the idea altogether. Their dream did not materialise. On reflection, however, one feels that it was probably a sensible decision, because BRM began to have serious difficulties with their own cars and engines, and, of course, the problems associated with qualifying a Formula One car multiplied with the years.

Sadly, alas, for similar reasons the Formula Three G19 was also abandoned. One car did approach completion and this was again a continuation of the G17/18 theme, but using a stronger chassis and a modified body to allow a BRM V8 2-litre power unit to be squeezed in.

So there ended the Formula single-seater programme, and the brothers decided, instead, to surge ahead with their road cars. But the project was not without its success; privately entered Ginetta G18s gained occasional creditable results, whilst the

Gurston Down 1970—Peter Voigt braking for Karousel—another class win

96

Ginetta G17, especially in the hands of Peter Voigt, was incredibly successful in hillclimbing events.

Peter Voigt had successfully campaigned a 998cc Imp DRW during 1968 and 1969, when he decided that he would sell the DRW less its engine and gearbox, and purchase a Ginetta G17 to which the engine and gearbox could be transferred. The engine he used was a full-race Nathan unit that gave in the region of 95 bhp.

When the car was ready, Peter entered his first event in the Ginetta in April 1970, at Brunton hillclimb, where he achieved a first in class. Two more events during April, at Harewood and Loton Park,

saw Peter and his G17 gain two more firsts in its class. And so it continued for the remainder of the season, with never less than a second placing. Twenty-one events in the Ginetta showed fourteen firsts, five seconds and two FTDs, with records at Thruxton (sprint), where he set one of his FTDs and a new course record, Prescott, Valance (the other FTD and another new course record), Oliver's Mount, Harewood, Great Auclum, Pontypool and Shelsley Walsh.

Pontypool 1970— Peter at Esses— another class win and 2nd FTD

Peter again with G17 now sporting aerodynamic aids

Peter and G17 again, another win

For the following, 1971, season Peter had made some alterations to his Ginetta. A deal was struck with Team Hartwell of Bournemouth who raised the power output of the engine to 100 bhp, but with a large sacrifice in the engine's torque, whilst Peter redesigned the engine/gearbox mountings, strengthened the roll-over hoop with additional stays, and added some aerofoil wings.

For his second, and final, season in the Ginetta, Peter was once again very successful. The first event at Pontypool hillclimb resulted in an FTD. The following sixteen events that season resulted in seven firsts, four seconds, two thirds and a further three FTDs, with records at Valance, Doune, Harewood and Cadwell Park. Peter then sold his Ginetta G17 which in his hands had been ultra-reliable: he had retired only once, and had used the same set of Dunlop tyres throughout both seasons!

G17 showing the chassis frame and detachable nose

The very modified, very attractive, G17 of Richard Homer

Today, the ex-Peter Voigt G17 is still campaigned on the hills, albeit in a much modified form, in the hands of its owner, Richard Homer. During 1982, Richard gained a first in class award at Harewood, and has had numerous second and third class awards at various venues.

*G18 cornering at
Brands Hatch*

*Rare sight of what
could have been
the G19, with its
BRM V8 engine just
noticeable*

Chapter Eleven

SOPHISTICATED SPORTS COUPÉ

Ginetta G21 (1970–1978)

THE 1970 London Motor Show saw the Ginetta company taking what appeared to be considerable steps forward, by displaying two prototypes of their forthcoming new model, the Ginetta G21. In some respects this new model looked not unlike a much larger version of the G15, albeit with a front-mounted engine.

Of the two examples exhibited, one was powered by a Ford 3-litre V6 engine, coupled to a standard 3-litre Ford gearbox, giving 137 bhp at 4,750 rpm, with the added option of either an overdrive installation or an automatic Borg-Warner transmission, if required. A Salisbury Power-Lok limited-slip differential, using a high final-drive ratio of 2.88-1, was used at the rear of the car.

The rear suspension was really rather special, somewhat similar to that used on the E-type Jaguar: attached to the base of the Ginetta-designed magnesium alloy hub-carriers were two lower parallel links to form wishbones, whilst the upper links were formed by the fixed length driveshafts, both of which had inboard and outboard universal joints. Four coil-spring/damper units were fitted, one unit either side of each driveshaft, attached at the base to the lower links and at the top end to a chassis subframe. The inner ends of the lower links were fixed to another subframe with the differential bolted immediately between these two subframes. To insulate any noise that may have been transmitted from this installation, the two subframes were mounted to the chassis by means of rubber Metalistic bushes. Non-parallel upper and lower trailing arms were also fitted.

The brakes on the rear utilised 10.4-inch diameter discs, mounted inboard, with the calipers actually bolted to the differential housing. The front discs were of 9.7-inch diameter. Another interesting feature of this 3-litre example was its electrically oper-

Because it was much larger than the G15, the G21 was being labelled as a two-plus-two by its audience at the Show, but although there was adequate space behind the seats for two small children, to all intent and purpose, the Ginetta G21 was purely a 2-seater sports coupé.

The G21 followed the same basic principles as most of its Ginetta predecessors. On this occasion using a full-length chassis made from 2-inch square section steel tube of 14, 15 and 16 gauge and a glassfibre body bolted to the chassis à la G15. The torsional rigidity of the G21 was increased by the use of 16 gauge sheet steel section to form the transmission tunnel, and this gave an appearance of a 'backbone chassis'.

At the close of the 1970 Motor Show the G21, although very well received — it actually received the acclaim of 'best car at the show' — it was much to the surprise and delight of the Walkletts that it was the smaller G15, also on show, that had attracted the more substantial orders. So the Walkletts' conclusion was evident: production of the G21 would have to be held over for the time being and resources concentrated instead on the G15. In any case, their Witham premises were far too small to cope with production of both models.

It was for these reasons, and looking to the future, of course, that the company began their search for larger premises. These were finally found when they moved to the new, larger factory at Sudbury in

ated door windows, and a special one-off radiator to cope with the cooling of this powerful engine.

The companion prototype featured a Ford 1599cc crossflow, overhead-valve engine (as used in the Ford Capri 1600 GT) giving some 84 bhp. This version too had independent suspension, but this time with a Ford 3.7-1 ratio live rear axle, with disc-brakes fitted at the front and conventional drum brakes used at the rear. Both versions used Triumph Vitesse steering and popular double wishbone and coil-spring/damper units for the front suspension, with a 5/8-inch anti-roll bar. Also fitted were 5½ x 13-inch Dunlop alloy wheels. Externally, the glass-fibre bodies of both prototypes were identical, but for one distinguishing factor: a much larger power bulge on the bonnet of the 3-litre version.

Suffolk in March of 1972. By this time the G21 had still presented itself only in its prototype forms, but during this period development of the G21 had progressed behind the scenes, in usual Ginetta style, whilst production of the G15 had continued.

Settled in their new spacious Sudbury factory, the Walkletts prepared for the second launch of the Ginetta G21 at the 1972 London Motor Show. It had now become evident that the company was concentrating fully on road cars. Although the Ford 3-litre version of the G21 appeared again at the Show, the Ford 1600cc engine version had been replaced by one with a Chrysler Rapier engine. The decision for the change had come about because the Chrysler engine gave a choice of either the standard 1725cc Rapier unit, or the more powerful 1725cc Holbay-tuned Rapier H120 (and later Hunter GLS) engine to be used. Also available for use with these engines was a Laycock-de Normanville overdrive. This was a distinct advantage over the smaller Ford engine for which no overdrive was available. A contributory factor to this change of manufacturer may have been Ginetta's already close liaison with the Chrysler company who supplied the engines, gearboxes and suspension components for the G15. At this time there was also a trend towards fitting larger capacity engines.

One major change from that of previous Ginettas was that the G21 would be sold only in its fully built form, and this is exactly how all G21s were sold.

Bob Walklett poses proudly by a G21 outside the new Ginetta factory at Sudbury

Despite this, Ginetta were, and still are, labelled only as kit-car manufacturers which is somewhat unfair.

At the Show on this occasion, the G21 got the response it deserved. But even this time production did not get under way immediately. In fact, it was not until September 1973 that production actually commenced. The delay on this occasion had occurred because both the G15 and the G21 were obliged to undergo statutory crash tests at the MIRA (Motor Industry Research Association) testing centre at Nuneaton, in Warwickshire. This was to comply with new government legislation on vehicle safety.

As it turned out, this hold-up proved to be no real setback whatsoever: in fact it probably helped increase sales. The reason for this was that the G21 (a 3-litre version) actually yielded one of the best results that had been seen at MIRA. The 30 mph impact into a brick wall had been sufficient to lift the rear wheels of the G21 some six inches off the ground, yet the car's steering wheel had moved back only 1¼ inches — the maximum allowed was 4 inches — and both doors could still be opened and shut in the normal manner, thus giving one hundred per cent cockpit integrity. This led the company to advertise in a manner to which they had not

G21 undergoing statutory crash test at MIRA— one of the best results seen there

been accustomed. Their full-page advertisements declaring 'Ginetta move into top gear for 1973' appeared in March of that year in certain motoring magazines, illustrating the G15 Series IV (as already covered in chapter 8) and also the G21, priced at £1875.

Despite the introduction of VAT, orders for both cars still came in at a reasonable level. But, in common with the majority of other manufacturers, the Walkletts could not have foreseen the impending oil crisis and subsequent economic recession that was to follow during that forthcoming winter. This crisis resulted in the escalation of the costs of raw materials and parts and consequently fewer orders for their cars. Obviously feeling the pinch from these increases, the company had to take some drastic action if it were to survive. Already, many small firms had begun to go to the wall. So it was reluctantly decided to drop the attractive little G15 and concentrate solely on the new model, the G21.

With G15 production now ended it was obvious that the Sudbury factory could not be economical to

G21 mould and its master jig. The body and floor are layed up separately and then laminated together

run for one model alone. Therefore, rather than struggle on to inevitable disaster, the Walkletts decided to cut their losses and return to their old Witham premises and concentrate on the G21 production there. As already mentioned, many firms were going bust at this time and, somehow, Ginetta inadvertently got mentioned in a motoring periodical amongst a list of bankrupt motor companies, at around the same time that they closed down their Sudbury factory. This very unfortunate error caused untold embarrassment, and even financial loss, to the Walkletts, because some potential customers and suppliers got cold feet.

Despite the gloom, however, Ginetta weathered the storm clouds that hung over so many small firms during those — fateful for many — melancholy months of 1974. Emerging not totally unscathed, but full of spirit, the company once again pushed the G21 and it was not long before the sales began to pick up. The prospects looked promising — and so they should have — for the G21 was, and still is, a very fine sports car. Word got around and the G21 started to receive enthusiastic reviews in the motoring magazines; even a very popular Sunday newspaper was to give the car a very creditable write-up.

During the latter months of 1974, the G21 got a good response. The Holbay-tuned engine version, known simply as the G21'S', and equipped with overdrive as standard, was selling at £2,598, whilst the G21 (overdrive being an option) sold at £2,196. It was at this time that the latter version was occupying the enviable position of being the least expensive specialist sports car on the market, thus making it excellent value for money. The much larger Ford 3-litre engine, all-independent-suspension version, which had been basically to special order only, had not been pursued with any vigour and the escalating costs for certain components in the prevailing economic climate had pushed its selling price to nearly £3,000. It was not long before the G21 3-litre was dropped altogether.

By the middle of 1976, the costs of the G21 and G21S had both risen dramatically, with the latter selling at no less than £3,496 inclusive of special car tax and VAT. The standard G21, however, was a remarkable £808 less than this price, and was deemed in some quarters to be a much better buy — but in its 'S' form the G21 was a very well equipped car. Strangely, this did not seem to deter the sales of either model, both proving to be equally popular.

The appearance of the G21 had not altered since its inception; minor detail changes to the door handles, replaced by Marina-type handles, and stylish Exacton alloy wheels, fitted in preference to the earlier Dunlop items, were the only external differences. As with the Ginetta G15, the front and rear bumpers fitted to the G21 originated from the same sources: the Volkswagen Beetle and the Riley Elf.

G21 steel chassis awaiting its glassfibre body

G21 bodies and chassis's in various stages of assembly

Smart and efficient, that's the G21 cockpit

On the G21, however, the rear Riley Elf bumper was cut and divided by the fitment of two number-plate lamps and the number plate itself. The stop/tail lights and indicators emanated from the Hillman Imp, as did the boot hinges and the external bonnet release handles. With the latter released, the entire front body section, front-hinged, could be lifted to give excellent engine acessibility. By further removing two bolts and disconnection of the wiring harness in this locality, the front body section could be removed completely.

In the typical Ginetta tradition of giving customers value for money, the specification of the G21 was, indeed, comprehensive. Such items as reclining front seats, real-leather-rimmed steering wheel,

laminated front screen, alloy wheels, seat belts and halogen headlamps — all normally regarded as extras — came as standard fitments. Amongst optional extras were a folding sunroof, heated rear screen (actually emanating from the MGB), tinted front laminated screen, radio and cassette player.

The interior of the G21 was finished to high standards: the reclining seats were trimmed in a cloth upholstery and had a wide range of fore and aft adjustment. The fascia panel was trimmed in a black vinyl and well hooded to restrict any annoying reflections in the windscreen at night from the full array of instrumentation, which included 140 mph speedometer, tachometer and further gauges for fuel, oil-pressure, water temperature and battery condition, all black-faced for anti-glare. Fascia-level fresh-air ventilation was from two eyeball inlets, one at either end of the fascia, and was made extremely effective by two outlets positioned behind both of the rear side-screens. Heating and demisting was taken care of by the use of a Triumph GT6 heater unit to which the intake of air came from a grill (of Jaguar XJ6 origin) sited behind the front bonnet section in front of the windscreen. The output was assisted by a 2-speed fan controlled by one of the seven rocker switches on the fascia. The remaining six rocker switches took care of the rear screen heater, the (2-speed) wipers, the screen-washer, the panel lights, the sidelights and the headlights. The indicators, horn and headlamp flasher/dip/main

G21 at Hindhead kit-car rally

beam, were all controlled by one stalk on the right hand side of the steering column, whilst a second stalk, on the left hand side was for the electrically operated overdrive, if fitted. The G21 also boasted a combined ignition/steering lock, high quality short pile wall-to-wall carpeting and a full headlining in a grey cloth. Dividing the two seats was a high transmission tunnel with a centre console, but there was no room for the handbrake here: instead this was placed on the right side of the driver.

Internal space inside the G21 allowed very little stowage in the front of the car: only a minuscule cosmetic glove-box on the fascia and a couple of bin-type pockets on the doors. Behind the seats, however, was enough space for a reasonable amount of luggage, or by the nature of its padded rear bulkhead and twin footwells, two small children could be accommodated, as already mentioned. The boot of the Ginetta G21 was largely taken up by the spare wheel, which sat upright on the left side, and the underfloor 10-gallon fuel tank, which itself was filled through a large flip-up-type filler cap sited on the outside of the rear wing.

Completed G21s at Sudbury

Nonetheless, the rectangular boot would accept a medium-sized suitcase and further soft baggage.

As far as performance went, the G21 was no slouch. Even when using the basic 1725cc Rapier engine, which was sited well back in the chassis frame to give the car a good balance, the G21 had a top speed of 112 mph and could accelerate from 0-60 in a time of 9.7 seconds, developing 79 bhp at 5,200 rpm. This engine had a compression ratio of 9.2–1 and used twin Stromberg carburettors and a standard Rapier, all-synchromesh, four-speed gearbox with a 3.7–1 ratio final drive (a 3.9–1 ratio differential was available as an option). A reasonably light weight of only 15 cwt and its clean, sleek, aerodynamic lines obviously helped contribute to the performance and economy — 35 mpg being the norm — of the G21.

The G21 'S', however, was certainly in the high performance bracket. Its more powerful Holbay H120 version of the Rapier engine, breathing through two twin-choke 40DCOE Weber carburettors, had some 95 bhp on tap and with the added extra of overdrive enabled the car to achieve a top speed of 120 mph and a 0-60 mph acceleration time of 8.5 seconds. By using the optional lower final-drive ratio of 3.9–1, the 0-60 mph acceleration time could be reduced to well under 8 seconds. Albeit a very fast sports car, the G21S could, nonetheless, still attain respectable fuel consumption figures of around 30 mpg, due in part again to a combination

Rear view of a G21—in this case the immaculate example owned by Kevin Bell

of excellent power-to-weight ratio and low drag factor, and, of course, the overdrive unit that was fitted as standard on the 'S' version: at 70 mph in top gear, in overdrive, the Holbay engine was turning at only a modest 2,800 rpm. The cooling of both variants of the G21 was taken care of by a front-mounted radiator of Ford Zephyr Six origin, suitably modified by Ginetta to fit.

111

A very smart G21S, owned by Kevin Bell

G21 accelerating with some verve

Out on the road the G21 tended to have some oversteer characteristics, but in the main was fairly neutral and a very controllable car, with its light and accurate rack and pinion steering (partly acquired from the Triumph GT6) which allowed its incredible lock enabling the G21 to be turned round in very narrow roads. The braking system of front discs and rear drums proved to be fade-free and would stop the car very effectively under all conditions. The G21 had tenacious road-holding qualities and precise handling — not equal to its predecessor, the G15 perhaps, but nonetheless superior to cars of similar specification. The ride was firm, but was well damped and similar to most other specialist cars: some acceptable kick-back could be felt through the steering column on imperfect roads. For those buyers who preferred an even firmer ride, Ginetta stocked a supply of alternative springs and adjustable dampers, and would fit these if required.

With the demise of the Ginetta G15, the G21 continued to be the sole production Ginetta model and continued as such until very late into 1978, after which it was phased out of production. The Ginetta G21 was a successful car, but curiously during its several years of production only 150 or so cars were ever built. It should, of course, have sold in much larger numbers and probably would have done had it not been for the Yom Kippur war and the economic recession.

Chapter Twelve

SPORTS 2000 RACER

Ginetta G22 (1978–1979)

AFTER what seemed like an eternity since Ginetta themselves had raced a works car, the Walkletts decided that it was time they returned again to the competition arena. Together they looked at the formulae and, having a preference for closed-in wheels, chose Sports 2000, a relatively new form in motor racing that appeared to be growing in popularity.

Development of a new car had began in earnest around the latter months of 1977. Within twelve months from the initial designs, a finished body/chassis was ready, awaiting its new 2-litre engine and Hewland gearbox, plus other necessary components. Comprising front and rear tubular steel subframes, the new Ginetta racer was designated the G22 — it differed from all previous models inasmuch as it was in no way influenced by any of the existing Ginetta designs.

Work progressed with the preparation of the G22 over the winter months of 1978: the Walkletts had every intention of having the car ready for the following season to enter in the Lola-dominated Sports 2000 championship. Last-minute development on the car, however, meant that unfortunately the coming season would not see the début of the G22. This typified the whole Ginetta philosophy: always caution, never doing anything in haste and above all, striving to get it *right*. The Walkletts feel it's no good building a racing car if it won't win races — come second and you've lost as far as they are concerned. If they put out a works car, then it has to be capable of winning outright. Their attitude is that nobody will buy a racing car that can only manage second…but win a race and you can be assured of customers. From this it can be said that if a Ginetta works car appears on the race circuit, it has to be fully competitive and it will be *right*.

Whilst preparation of the G22 was continuing,

superb at speed through the slower bends of the circuit. The same could not be said, however, about its handling on the faster bends. After some deliberation, the Walkletts decided on some small aerodynamic aids to the rear of the body, and these in effect cured the handling problems on the fast bends, but unhappily led to other problems on the straight, when full power was required.

Rear view of John Knapton's G22

Enthusiast, John Knapton's G22 receiving some enquiring looks in somewhat unfamiliar surroundings

two more body/chassis units were made and assembled, because the company had already received enquiries for replicas. At last the G22 works car was completed and ready to be put through its paces. Two very experienced drivers, Syd Fox and Phil Dowsett, were enlisted to test the G22 extensively. The testing took place on a local race circuit and some areas of the G22 performance were described ecstatically by the two drivers — Syd Fox is said to have described the 140 mph car as absolutely

The months continued with the G22 being dogged by further problems like those mentioned, but eventually the car was nearing the perfection required by the Walkletts. Unfortunately, the pursuit of perfection had meant that another season had passed and there was now a doubt amongst the brothers whether the Sports 2000 category had been a wise choice. The development of the G22 had held the Walkletts plans up somewhat, but it was imperative that the car was competitive. However, they got the impression that other makes were not doing as well as expected in Sports 2000 — the grids also were not filling as had been anticipated. Reservations began to creep in as to whether the G22 would now be a viable proposition as far as sales of the car were concerned. The Walkletts saw no point in racing a car in a category where grids were not full, and in any case they now had another new car on the cards and decided that perhaps it would be best to call a halt to the G22 altogether. Again, this typified the whole Ginetta approach — never could the brothers be accused of being impetuous. If the G22 had been entered in the Sports 2000 races, perhaps it would have been successful: but that would not have been regarded as being in true Ginetta style. The G22 project was eventually halted.

One could say that of all the Ginettas ever built the G22 was perhaps the least successful commercially, and that the time and money spent on it might have been better spent in a different way — by concentrating instead, for example, on the project on which they were about to embark. On the other hand it is true that the design of the G22 clearly showed the ingenuity of this small and skilful company, and the ability of the partners to turn their hands to a variety of design problems; in common with all Ginettas, the G22 was an attractive looking car. It is regrettable that it did not appear on the grids: it was undeniably an authentic Ginetta model — there would have been no mistaking the car amongst the majority of other, almost indistinguishable, Sports 2000 racers.

The G22 works car, with its flush rear end, wide arches flowing forward to its shovel nose, strategically positioned air-intakes and neat, but substantial, roll-over bar, remains in the factory showroom at Witham today: the other two uncompleted cars have been sold to Ginetta enthusiasts. One of them is now completed and ready to double up as a hill-climb/sprint car.

The Walklett brothers had had in mind plans to develop a new single-seater, along similar lines to the G22, if the latter had been successful, but in any case at this stage of the game they realised that the costs of any form of motor racing were growing to such proportions that, as far as Ginetta were concerned, they really were prohibitive. Their attention, therefore, had to be diversified back to road cars.

Chapter Thirteen

LOOKING FORWARD

Ginetta G23 and G24 (1980–

DURING the latter part of the 1970s and early part of 1980 the Walkletts, not having produced cars in a large enough number to sustain a regular income, derived their livelihood, in the main, from renovation and servicing of customers' cars, and also by selling refurbished secondhand Ginettas. As always, the demand for spares, be it a brake hose or a body panel, ran at a consistently high level. The majority of moulds from previous models have been kept over the years, ensuring a reliable source of supply for panels for all but a few of the very early Ginetta models. Demand, in fact, in all areas, was such that the company could probably continue to survive on this alone, but that really wouldn't be Ginetta policy.

The attempt to return to racing a works car had failed, and since during the past few years, the company had kept a lower profile than even they were accustomed to maintain, one could have been forgiven for thinking that Ginetta had disappeared altogether.

Early in 1980 it had been rumoured that the Walkletts were planning to announce a new road-going sports coupé. What came about, however, was a complete and unexpected surprise: not one, but two new prototypes were announced by the company. To cap this there was further speculation that the introduction of a new road-version of one of the company's famous racing cars was also imminent.

The first of the two prototypes was in fact a coupé derivative of the Ginetta G21, featuring the same tried and trusted Chrysler (now Talbot) 1725cc engine and mechanics, but fully revised and totally updated with a new streamlined front end that incorporated electronically-operated pop-up headlights and a subtle bib spoiler. A new matt-black-finish front bumper with integral side/indicator lamps was

117

The first picture of the G23 prototype

G23 with its smart hardtop in position and winking its pop-up headlamps in the Witham factory yard

added, and the scuttle was infinitely smoother, with the area around the door windows and rear side-screens also cleaned up by the removal of the previously fitted, old-fashioned chrome trim. The view from the rear remained similar but updated with the addition of a new, deep bumper (again in matt-black) incorporating fog and reversing lights. The interior too, had been revised with more attention to detail. The final embellishment was achieved by the fitting of a set of the latest Exacton alloy wheels. The car was designated the G24.

If the G24 was to whet the appetites of Ginetta enthusiasts and the like, then the other prototype car, the G23 — an all-new model — was to be mouth-watering. A combination of a Ford 2.8-litre V6 engine (in carburettor form rather than fuel-injection) and strong, but light, glassfibre body with

a very rigid tubular steel frame chassis running the whole length of the car and out to the door sills, and in effect incorporating an additional backbone structure — the same chassis as for the G24, incidentally. This simply beautiful machine shared an identical front end with the G24, but its ultra-smooth lines flowed freely through to a completely new rear end that incorporated a deep boot, and it was in a convertible guise rather than a coupé. The weather-protection hood was of unique Ginetta design, fitting over a special moulded targa bar, which enclosed a hidden steel rollover bar, and a central stay that attached to the top of the front screen rail. A hardtop, finished in a very attractive vinyl covering, with unusual but very distinctive elliptical side windows, would be offered as an option.

The open-top G23 was claimed to be able to top 130 mph and to have acceleration in the region of 0–60 in only 6 seconds. It used a Ford live axle at the rear to match the power supply, whilst Ginetta had developed their own mountings at the rear to provide for the installation of rubber bush insulated coil springs and dampers mounted independently of each other, thus providing an uncompromising choice of rear spring ratings at the same time as all-round independent style suspension, without resorting to excessive cost.

Costs, of course, are of vast importance to any motor manufacturer and both of these prototypes were introduced at a time when another economic recession was about to bite. Ginetta would prefer to sell cars complete, but to do this would involve vast expense — and in no way can this be afforded. For companies like Ginetta, the only way round this dilemma is to offer the car for home assembly. The intention was to sell the cars as a complete body/chassis unit, with only the suspension, engine and gearbox to be fitted by the customer — the simplest way of selling a car that is, to all intent and purpose, factory-built. A pre-production G23 body/chassis had already been prepared.

Details of the G23 and G24 models, both of which would have stood any major manufacturer in

Steve Newport's beautiful G23

119

high stead, were published in several motoring periodicals during the latter months of 1980.

By 1981 the recession in the motor industry in general was deepening, with sales of all cars being hit hard, so caution once again crept into the Ginetta domain. With many people feeling the pinch, the Walkletts had to consider whether to continue with their new models or to mark time. A market for this

Identical front of the G24 to the G23

Alternative Cars Ltd

Alternative Cars Ltd

type of specialist car existed, of course, — the classic British sports car was a breed fast becoming extinct — but rather than rush ahead the Walkletts, in usual style, decided to postpone pursuance of the G23/G24 until the economic climate was more propitious.

The situation was reviewed constantly. There appeared to be growing signs of a kit-car revival, backed up with the introduction of one or two specialist magazines devoted entirely to the subject of alternative vehicles. Whilst this boom appeared to grow, the other side of the picture was the lament-

121

able finale to all forms of mass-production sports cars in the UK: the closure of the MG factory at Abingdon signalled the death-knell for this long established and famous marque. And with the Triumph Spitfire already killed off, came the sad news that the only surviving British volume production sports car, the Triumph TR7, was to meet the same pathetic end by September of 1981.

With virtually no 'cheap' sports cars available —

the only exception being the Fiat X19 perhaps — and since one-time Ginetta rivals, Lotus and TVR, had both gone distinctly up-market, a very large gap appeared in the market. The Walkletts saw this gap as an invitation to launch a revamped version of one of their earlier models, in the hope that it would bring in the 'bread and butter' money to permit them to tool up for production of the G23/G24, if required.

Chapter Fourteen

RESURRECTION OF THE '4'

Ginetta G4 Series IV (1981–

THE demise of the MGB, the MG Midget and the Triumph Spitfire — coupled with the news of a similar fate for the TR7 — was lamentable. Seldom had such a large gap appeared in any part of the car market, so prospects looked good for the introduction of a low-cost sports car, in a price range below that of the Fiat X19, which would now occupy the niche of being the only reasonably priced sports car coming from the major manufacturers. Only a specialist manufacturer could possibly produce a car selling at a price below that of the Fiat and even that specialist would have to market the car in component, or kit-form.

The Walkletts had given much thought to the situation, and concluded that perhaps the resurrection of the Ginetta G4 — but this time with the accent on road use only, and in an updated guise — would be able to get the company some much-needed sales. The G4 had the right reputation with

its proven competition background — it was a real sports car. So the old G4 jigs and moulds were dusted down and plans for its rejuvenation went firmly ahead. A new chassis, using 1-, 1½- and 2-inch square section steel tube , was made, based upon the G4 Series III chassis. It was imperative that the new G4 had more room available to enable it to meet modern-day requirements — the original G4 would have been too cramped for today's standards — so the new body was lengthened by some 3 inches and the width by 2 inches. This gave more leeway for enlarging the cockpit and increasing the boot area. The front section now appeared to look longer, with the bonnet finishing below the door line. At the rear the wings are still pronounced, but look much less so from immediately behind the car, chiefly because of a revamped rear end and larger, more level looking, boot lid. The glassfibre reinforced body is bolted to the new chassis. The prototype G4 Series IV was ready to be unveiled at the beginning of January 1981.

First impressions given by the new Series IV G4 were shades of a Chevrolet Corvette, depending upon the direction from which one looked at the extremely curvaceous car. It is a somewhat curious looking car, but certainly does not look unpleasant — from some angles it does indeed look very stylish,

The G4, Series 4, on the day it was unveiled in the Ginetta showroom

especially the side view: the lines of the car flow gracefully from the front to the rear. The front view, however, does tend to be slightly disturbing because of its bulbous appearance; but there is no doubting that it has the essential Ginetta hallmark.

The prototype G4 Series IV used a neat arrangement to enable the black vynide hood to be fitted. This consisted of a sturdy roll-over bar, which was met by a moulded T-bar coming from the top of the

deep front screen header panel. To actually erect the hood is somewhat laborious: first the 'flying buttresses' have to be bolted in place, then the hood frame must be slotted into the roll-over bar before the hood can be stretched and fastened. Although apparently tedious, it is well-designed and, once fitted, does not flap at speed or leak during wet weather. With the (laminated) front screen pillars steel reinforced, full roll-over protection was provided. The door sidescreens were permanent fixtures. Pop-up headlights were employed and there were individual housings for the indicators and sidelights, and in the middle of the bonnet was a combined power bulge/air scoop. The prototype was fitted with a Ford 2-litre single-overhead-cam

125

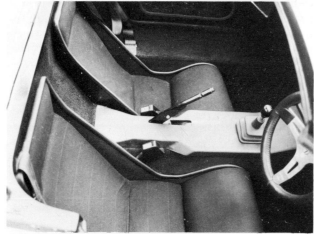

Alternative Cars Ltd

Pinto engine, and was reported exclusively in one of the specialist car magazines.

The Walklett brothers' aim was to sell the car as a 'main assembly', which meant that the customer would purchase a completed body/chassis unit, selling at £1,795 plus VAT. The 'main assembly' consisted of the complete glassfibre body, including fitted boot, bonnet (front hinged for easy access to the engine compartment) and doors, bolted to the full-length steel chassis. Clutch/brake/accelerator pedal assembly were fitted, together with all brake piping and master cylinders. All wiring, lights, indicators were fitted and working (the battery was supplied). The steering column complete with leather-rim steering wheel and indicator stalk were fitted, as were all instruments, wiper motor, arms and blades, and washer, fuel tank, fuel lines and handbrake assembly. The cockpit interior was fully trimmed and carpeted, with seats and seat belts fitted. Finally the body was painted in the colour of the customer's choice.

The Walkletts saw this 'main assembly' package completely eliminating the need for any professional knowledge: the customer got a car that was finished to factory standards, and required only the suspension assemblies, the engine/gearbox, and wheels to be fitted to complete the car. Also this self-build principle gave the buyer plenty of scope for choice, enabling the car to be completed in just a few days, or — if finances would not allow this —

then parts could be ordered when required and the car put together over a longer period of time.

Within a matter of only a few months, Ginetta had revised the new G4 in the area of the front bonnet section. Gone were the pop-up headlights, and the sidelights disappeared too, replaced by a fixed headlight/sidelight combination: these changes had to be made so that the headlamps could be raised in order to comply with Construction and Use regulations. When the car later appeared in photographs accompanying reports on road tests in several motoring periodicals, the air-intake/bulge on the bonnet had been replaced by an air-outlet/bulge which had been dramatically increased in size.

Inside the G4 Series IV, the interior is uncluttered and very efficient looking. There is a thick leather-rimmed steering wheel, with a simple, but well-designed and laid out fascia — trimmed in leather-cloth — and all the necessary instruments and switches are to hand. The seats are Ginetta-designed, and although these are in a fixed position people of most shapes and sizes can be accommodated.

On the road, especially in the 2-litre guise, the G4 Series IV is a flyer! It offers all the exhilarating performance that a sports car driver could ask for. With an all-up weight of only 13 cwt, the G4 produces 98 bhp at 5,800 rpm with the 2-litre engine fitted. Using a Ford rear axle with a ratio of 3.09–1, 0–60 mph comes up in around 7 seconds and is matched with a top speed of 115 mph, and surprisingly, with very little adverse effect on economy — the G4 producing commendable fuel consumption figures of between 30 and 35 mpg. The 8½-gallon fuel tank is situated in the boot — as also, unfortunately, is the filler, making it none to easy to replenish.

Because the exhaust expires from the driver's door sill, the G4 Series IV is a rather noisy car, especially at speed, but the cockpit is snug with both driver and passenger fitting in comfortably between the large transmission tunnel and the very deep (steel-reinforced) sills, with plenty of elbow room and safety protection.

G4 with hood up

Braking is in the usual Ginetta style of front discs and rear drums, with no servo fitted: it requires high pedal pressure, but at the same time it is nicely progressive, with no hint of fade.

Since the G4 in its Series IV form was re-introduced at the start of 1981, orders for the car have continued to date, though at a level slightly lower than was originally anticipated.

Side-view of a later G4 Series 4 with even more humps!

Goes like a train—and it does, the very fast G4 Series 4

Alternative Cars Ltd

Chapter Fifteen

THE WAY AHEAD

Ginetta GRS and G25 (1982–

IN common with the large part of the Ginetta story so far, it must be true to say that there is very little time, if any, ever wasted behind the scenes at Ginetta Cars Ltd, whereas the impression one gets, on the outside, is the exact opposite — that there is very little activity at all. The ancient, presumably defunct, petrol pumps outside the Witham works make the premises look anything but as up-to-date as the products that emerge from it, and with such consistent regularity.

A classic example to prove the point came during the latter part of 1982, when the new G4 Series IV appeared to be receiving all the attention. Not having appeared at the Motor Show for nigh on a decade, the Walkletts suddenly, out of the blue, made a surprise appearance at the October 1982 Motor Show held at the National Exhibition Centre, Birmingham. And their exhibit was even more of a surprise: it was not under the Ginetta banner but

under GRS. Named the GRS Tora, the vehicle was not a sports car but a five-seater leisure vehicle, looking everything like a cross between a Range Rover and a Talbot Matra-Rancho. The GRS, proving to be extremely popular, had the Walklett brothers rushed off their feet. One enthusiast even put in an order before the doors of the NEC could be opened! And in true Ginetta style the Walkletts did not trailer the GRS to the Show... they actually drove it there!

But what had caused the brothers to diversify like this? Simply, they had envisaged the kit-car explosion which is now taking place, and it was missing a vehicle of the stature and quality of the GRS. Many, many months of thought and work have gone into the GRS, and at a price of only £1,275 (fully inclusive of VAT) it is extremely good value. It is supplied in kit-form, relying entirely on components from the Hillman Hunter range — a previously

untapped source for parts for kit-cars. From the
excellent reports being given to the GRS and with
the order book filling daily, there is no doubt that it
is going to be a real success.

Then what of the Ginetta as a sports car? Well, the
answer to that — although it seems almost inconceivable — is that since 1981 the Walkletts have
been working on a replacement for their best-seller,
the G15. Development has steadily progressed on
this newest and latest Ginetta, which will be designated the G25. Although as yet nothing has been
finalised, a prototype has been built and description
of this is best left to the accompanying photographs.

The GRS Tora—
versatile 5-seater
total utility and
leisure vehicle.
Available for home
assembly and takes
components from
the Hillman Hunter
range of vehicles

Since the success of the G15, for which a strong demand still exists at prices well-above those originally paid, Ginetta Cars have been keen to return to this market with a functional mid-engine coupé of the 1980s.

In choosing the Ford Fiesta parts and installing the engine in the rear, the G25 design meets all the requirements of modern needs; both in 950cc form for 50 mpg and up to 1600cc turbo for sheer performance.

After gaining a vast amount of insight into the motoring public from their discussions and general conversations at the October 1982 Motor Show, the Walklett brothers know now, more than ever, that enthusiasts are more competent to bolt together vehicles bought in kit-form; and, more important, they know quality when they see it. Given a fully engineered body/chassis, the enthusiast can do the rest with no problems.

When the wraps are officially taken of the new Ginetta, it will probably be a revelation — it will, of course, be in a component form, but above all else it can be guaranteed that it will be excellent value for money. The end result is intended to be an ultra-modern sports car, and by judging the prototype, this aim will be achieved easily. The Walkletts see this method of selling specialist cars as the way ahead. What could be more simpler than to transfer all the standard suspension assemblies and running gear from a base vehicle — in this case a Ford Fiesta — to a fully engineered body/chassis unit?

Of all the projects the Walkletts have embarked upon, the forthcoming Ginetta is probably the most ambitious. And, incidentally, if it is mid-engined, as the prototype is, it will be the first real British mid-engined road car since the Lotus Europa and the AC 3000. Another fine sports car designed and built by Ivor Walklett and brothers, Bob, Trevor, and Douglas — undeniably, the most underrated designer and company in the UK, Ginetta Cars Ltd.

The Ginetta G25 will also be equally suitable for — competition — from circuit to rallycross.

A unique feature for those who are unable to afford all-new parts is that the G25 will be purchasable as a Ginetta body/chassis assembly, along with the special Ginetta parts, so that components from a used Fiesta can be transferred to complete

PHOTOGRAPHIC ACKNOWLEDGEMENTS

The author would like to thank the following photographers, agencies, magazines, motoring enthusiasts, friends and others, for allowing him the use of the photographs and illustrations featured in this book.

All uncredited photographs/illustrations are by the author

Alternative Cars Ltd, p 40 (bottom), 120, 121, 126 & 128 (top and bottom)
Autosport, p32
Harold Barker, p 25 (bottom), 72, 79
Phil Beevers, p 99
Paul Boothroyd, p 27 (bottom)
Derek Buckett, p 84, 85, 86 (bottom left), 92 (top)
Classic & Sportscar, p 2, 6, 7 (bottom), 24, 47, 57, 96, 97 (top)
Tony Clinkard, p 27 (top)
Campbells of Cheadle, Staffs, p 53
Alan Collins, p 73 (bottom)
Peter Cook, p 90 (top and bottom)
Peter 'Leigh' Davis, p 7 (top), 18 (top), 21 (top right), 23 (bottom right)
Hugo Dixon, p 125 (top right)
Malcolm Elston, p 10 (top left)
Armin Eigelsrieter, p 56 (top, left and right)
Neil Emery, p 127 (left)
'Focus 3' Photography, p 80 (top)

John Gaisford, p 73 (top), 75, 80 (bottom)
Ginetta Cars Limited, frontispiece, p 4, 8, 14, 16, 19 (bottom), 21 (bottom left), 22, 23 (top right), 36, 37, 44, 50, 56 (bottom), 58, 66, 98, 100 (left), 102, 104, 118 (left)
Donald Grant, p 98 (bottom left and right)
Steve Greensword, p 100 (right), 114, 124, 127, 131, 132, 133
Derek Hibbert, p 91
Ian Higgins, p 28 (top)
Ann Jones, p 78 (top)
Mike Kettlewell Collection, p 33, 34, 95 (left)
John Knapton, p 115 (left and right)
LAT Photographic, p 12, 17 (left and right), 18 (bottom), 19 (top), 20
Rod Leach, 'Nostalgia' p 38
Russell Madden, 39, 40 (top)
Bruno Meir, p 81 (bottom), 82
Adrian Moody, p 54
John Morris, p 10 (bottom), 11

Motoring News, p 49, 51, 86 (bottom right), 87, 92 (bottom)
Steve Newport, p 118 (right), 119, 122
G Paumann, p 25 (top), 26
Richard A Petit, p 59, 60, 61
George Ritchie, p 81 (top right)
Fred Scatley, p 27 (bottom), 28 (bottom), 29 (top), 45, 46, 74, 86 (top left), 88
Selwyn-Smith, Evan vi
Marcel Spiess, p 55 (top left and right)
Kaora Shinano, p 81 (top left)
H R S Spedding, p 95 (top right)
Colin Taylor Productions/Air India, p 31
Garry Taylor, p 76-77, 78 (bottom left)
Gerry Tyack, p 89
Thoroughbred and Classic Car, p 103, 105, 106, 107, 108 (left), 110, 112 (bottom)
Peter Voigt, p 94, 97 (bottom) 98 (top)
What Car?, p 67 (Top and Bottom), 68 (left and right), 70
Kay Williams, p 64

INDEX